MULTIFAMILY REAL ESTATE INVESTING

CREATE RELIABLE MONTHLY CASH FLOW, OUTPACE
INFLATION, AND DOMINATE WITH SMALL
MULTIFAMILY PROPERTIES, EVEN WITHOUT
EXPERIENCE

MORGAN LANE

CONTENTS

FREE GIFT

Dear Reader,

Thank you for purchasing my book! As a way of saying thank you, I've created a guide on *7 Massive Mistakes First Time Real Estate Investors Must Know To Avoid.*

Just Scan the QR code below to claim your gift!

INTRODUCTION

Real estate cannot be lost or stolen, nor can it be carried away. Purchased with common sense, paid for in full, and managed with reasonable care, it is about the safest investment in the world.

— FRANKLIN D. ROOSEVELT

In 1929, Americans were devastated to experience the worst market crash in the nation's history. What Americans didn't know at that time was that this crash would be the first of several over the next century.

A market crash can stimulate several different responses, but the most notable is panic. Investors sold shares upon shares of company stock to offset their losses. People took on multiple jobs and long work hours to increase their incomes, and homeowners sold their land and property.

During this experience, some looked ahead and saw an opportunity. As homeowners sold their homes out of fear or necessity, investors took the chance to buy real estate for cheap. As the market climbed out of its pit, investors now had something physical and safe to hold and investments to last and provide a reliable income stream.

When carefully considered, researched, and funded, real estate may be the most effective investment you will ever make.

YOUR MONEY IS NOT GUARANTEED

The 2008 financial crisis served as a wake-up call for the modern world. A little over eight years had passed since the "dot-com bubble" and over 20 years since the notorious Black Monday crash of 1987. All three of these economic disasters proved how easily they could severely disrupt a person's livelihood in a short amount of time.

But even when the economic climate is prosperous and promising, there is still no true security you can have in your job or your savings. Jobs can disappear suddenly without any indication. Factors like failing performance, downsizing, and organizational collapse can abruptly bring employment to an end. Global disruptions like wars, pandemics, and financial collapses can also influence job availability and the average income.

Savings are also not entirely reliable. Despite the historical belief that you should put money away for a "rainy day" or "in case of emergency," these nest eggs are only alive if you feed them with income. They are not sufficient to handle growing problems like inflation.

Inflation is an ongoing reality to be contended with, particularly when saving for the future. Inflation results as a response to the rise in demand for goods and services. The more consumers want a particular good or service, the more the price for that resource increases as producers increase the price.

Take an undergraduate degree, for example. A college education is arguably one of the costliest investments you can make. According to educationdata.org, an average public college 4-year degree cost $5,144 in 1963. In 1989, that same degree cost $52,982. Compare that to 2020, when the same degree costs $101,584.

Imagine that you spent years of hard work putting away money so that you could send your child to college. Even if you saved enough to send your child through all four years of college in 1989, that same amount would only take your child halfway through their college experience in 2020. The money you painstakingly put away for years no longer carries as much weight as it did. Due to inflation, your buying power every year will decrease. So, you find yourself trapped, every year chasing inflation and never feeling like you have enough money to accomplish your goals. The only way out of this pit is to break the cycle and find financial freedom.

FINDING FINANCIAL FREEDOM

Financial freedom is a genuine concept where you are no longer a slave to your current financial circumstances. You are in control and aware of where you can allocate your finances. You know how to develop a reliable cash flow that allows you to live the quality of life you desire. You no longer fear making financial decisions because you can prepare for any situation.

The answer lies in investments. Although saving is still a critical practice, investing will help you combat inflation and create that reliable cash flow.

Saving means that you will have money available whenever you need it. This money will only lose value due to inflation, but not because cash leaves your account. You will also be able to use a savings account to plan for events and goods you may be interested in getting soon.

On the other hand, **investment** is better for your long-term planning, like saving for college or retirement. Investments allow you the space to grow your money and gain more over time, but they also require more risk. You are using money to get more money potentially. Most people commonly think of the stock market when they think about investing. But there is another, more secure option.

Real Estate.

Potential investors commonly overlook this investment area, mainly because they don't realize its potential or know how to wield it properly. While stocks are much more straightforward and transactionally simple, real estate investment requires more significant financial and time investments and is much harder to liquidate.

However, real estate investing also has the capacity to provide excellent benefits. You can leverage homes for other investments. You can also choose to develop and sell houses for a profit, rent them out for a passive income stream, or sell the land to developers. This flexibility is only one of the advantages of investing in real estate.

You bought this book because you want to learn more about real estate. Maybe you're trying to develop a career, or, like many others, you've realized that market instability can quickly threaten your livelihood. Homes and buildings are tangible, and you can control them. What better way to build a relatively safe financial capital than investing in real estate?

Though you may be interested in various areas of real estate, one sector is widely underutilized: **Multifamily real estate**.

What is it, you ask? And how is it different from other investment instruments, you wonder?

The answer to your pressing questions awaits you in subsequent chapters. By the end, you will become well-versed in real estate investment challenges and have a clear path to building your wealth in the long run.

The only question that remains is: Are you ready?

PART - I - THE FIRST STEP TO FINANCIAL FREEDOM

1

WHAT IS REAL ESTATE INVESTMENT?

L et's start from the top. Real estate is any physical, tangible land or constructs that take up space, including every building and plot of land on the planet.

Real estate is unique because it is not digital or held in banks like stocks, bonds, and other investments. This property takes up actual space in the real world.

Even though real estate is physical and stationary, one can wield it in many ways. You can improve real estate and invest in building a structure or develop an already made structure. Investors can use this structure to create products, rent to tenants, or sell the whole structure to buyers.

How a property is utilized, maintained, and even owned plays a significant role in the surrounding economy. Likewise, the surrounding economy influences the property's value and income potential. For example, the environment directly surrounding the property can drastically change its value, even if maintained well. Homes in a well-maintained neighborhood will typically see a greater value than those in a community that is not well-maintained.

Understanding the environment is a crucial skill for a real estate investor. But a knowledgeable investor should also understand the type of property into which they are putting their money. The even more savvy investor will understand how to use their property type to their advantage.

TYPES OF REAL ESTATE

There are four main types of real estate: plots of land, residential, commercial, and industrial.

Each of these types plays a role in the real estate market. While we will primarily focus on the residential multifamily homes, you should also be aware of the other types of real estate out there.

Plots of Land

Even if you don't have a building established, any land you own is considered real estate. This land could be anything from a two-story apartment complex to an overgrown pocket of weeds in an abandoned town.

Most of the time, *plots (or pieces) of land refer to either vacant lots or working parcels*, like farms and ranches.

Selecting the right plot of land can be an excellent investment, especially if you foresee development happening in that region. Many investors have received an incredible offer from commercial developers for a simple plot of land that didn't cost them much to buy. Or their plot of land was in an ideal location to start a business, tiny home rental, or other enterprises.

Residential

Residential is the type of real estate most people think of when contemplating real estate, and we'll spend the most time discussing it in this book. Residential real estate, by definition, is any real estate that serves as a *living residence for a person or persons*. This type can include single-family homes, condominiums, multi-family homes, etc.

Residential real estate can be newly built homes or long-existing homes. They are generally meant for individuals and their families and are subject to the codes and standards of their neighborhood or county.

You can wield residential real estate in a variety of ways. One of the most common is buying a home and renting it out to tenants. Another option is to treat it as wholesale and market the rights to contract to potential investors.

Commercial

Commercial real estate has to do with any *land used for buying, selling, or marketing products.* If the property's primary purpose is business or service, it's commercial.

These products include hospitality, like hotels and apartments, and they can also include hospitals, churches, schools, and law offices.

Commercial real estate has its own set of rules and codes that it must abide by, based on the business or service. Commercial buildings are generally more expensive and require careful planning to utilize effectively. Most investors buy these properties and rent out the units to persons and businesses.

Industrial

Industrial real estate is primarily used for warehousing and manufacturing materials and storage or research facilities. Businesses or organizations often utilize industrial real estate for an auxiliary purpose. Many industrial real estate investors buy the properties intending to rent out the buildings to other companies and organizations or use the facilities for their own business ventures.

BEGINNERS IN PROPERTY BUYING

If you buy or sell property, you are investing in real estate. But this market can be complicated, full of legal jargon and rules. For example, when you are wholesaling, you aren't allowed to market the property itself; instead, you market the *rights to the contract* for the property.

See? The real estate arena can be very confusing and, for newcomers, daunting. But it is possible to navigate. People become real estate investors every day. But first, they must understand the ins and outs of the real estate market.

THE REAL ESTATE MARKET

When you think of the real estate market, what comes to mind?

For most people, it's an image of a realtor handing a set of keys over to a smiling couple. For others, they may imagine owning an apartment complex or buying expensive homes to resell. Usually, people think only of the seller and the buyer.

The real estate market consists of many different parts and roles. The market is full of people who manage properties, perform appraisals, construct new buildings, and provide legal counseling and education to investors. These jobs are essential to the market's growth and sustenance.

For this book, you need to understand the role of new constructions and the real estate agent. New structures are essential because they provide the buildings required for investors.

Suppose there is a decrease in new constructions. In that case, the market value of existing homes may go up as the housing demand increases (also known as a **seller's market**). If there is a boom in new constructs, market values of existing homes may go down (also known as a **buyer's market**).

In a seller's market, the seller has the advantage because prices are high, and buyers have less leverage to obtain a purchase price at their desired amount. The seller has the pricing power. In a buyer's market, the seller doesn't have as many options for selling the property and must be more willing to compromise with the buyer if they want to make money. So, the buyer has the pricing power. Keeping track of new constructions in the region is one way to read the real estate market.

It merits noting that the term **new construction** or "new home" usually refers to any residential real estate that has never been rented or occupied. These can be designer neighborhoods where buyers select from premade floor plans or a newly built house, including infills constructed on vacant or freshly cleared land.

Any homes that do not meet these criteria *should not advertise as new homes*, and you should be wary of those sellers. In rare situations, an extreme renovation on an existing property may qualify as a "new home." Still, you should investigate if you encounter this claim.

Real Estate Agents

Real estate agents are important figures in the real estate world. These professionals can direct you to some of the best places to find your next investment property and help you learn the market trends in that region. Even if you choose not to use them to find your properties, they are still great resources when trying to find potential buyers. It's in your best interest to get to know a few.

Understanding this market and its components are essential, especially since real estate trends often indicate how well the US economy is overall. If the economy is doing well, the number of new constructions and the amount of people buying and selling homes is usually high.

REAL ESTATE INVESTMENT

The real estate market is vast but breaking in is relatively simple—if you are willing to put in the work.

As mentioned before, there are many ways to invest in real estate. Still, the most common is to buy residential properties and either sell them for a profit (house-flipping, wholesaling, etc.) or rent them out (tenants, vacation homes, AirBnB, etc.).

In addition to these methods, real estate properties often "appreciate," meaning their value increases with the surrounding area. Due to this reality, many investors choose to "buy and hold." As a home's market value increases, a patient investor will have options. They can eventually sell the house for an increased price or pull equity (the amount you've paid back and own on the house) out as cash. They may then use this money to buy another or more properties, and this multiplies their income.

Other recent options for investing in real estate involve investments in the various stocks and bonds markets. One current investment option includes **Real Estate**

Investment Trusts (REITs), which allow investors to put money into a collection of real estate types held by a company. By putting money into this company, the investor earns money based on how well the properties owned by the company perform.

Another type of investment option is the Mortgage-Backed Securities (MBS). MBS allows investors to invest in a company that holds the rights to mortgages handed out by banks. As people pay on their mortgages, they pay the company which holds the mortgage note. Investors can benefit without putting in the work to sell or buy an actual loan.

When utilizing MBS, the investor buys the mortgage, so they get paid instead of the actual lender. The risk, however, is that if the mortgage-payer defaults, the investor won't get paid and could lose money.

This risk was a significant contribution to the 2008 economic crisis. Subprime borrowers—those paying higher interest rates due to low income—began to default on loans when the prices of homes started to increase. This situation resulted in the nonpayment of mortgages and, thus, financial losses. As these began to rise, the banks tried to navigate bad MBS. Still, these efforts failed, and eventually, the economy crumbled. Solely through the intervention of the U.S. Treasury and several strategic financial bailouts was the economy finally able to recover.

Mortgage-backed securities are still available; however, after the 2006-2008 MBS crisis, the government and banks have implemented measures to regulate the process. More people generally pay back their mortgages. Since then, this has been an excellent option for investors who want to break into the real estate investment world without managing their property.

That's a lot of information! Real estate seems like a promising investment, doesn't it? But how does it compare with other investment instruments, and how can it benefit you?

2

WHY INVEST IN REAL ESTATE?

Now that you have a basic understanding of real estate, we can explore this investment opportunity even more.

No particular type of person does better at real estate than others. There are many ways to approach real estate investment; anyone can succeed if they put forth the effort.

Perhaps you are someone who wants to invest in the physical property but doesn't want to deal with the maintenance or management. You could buy a property and hire a management company to invest in REITs for an even further "hands-off" approach.

Do you like working with your hands? Does the smell of wood, mortar, and power tools excite you? Then house-flipping or renovating may be something you want to investigate.

There are so many ways to go about investing in real estate. The only limit is your imagination and work ethic. Of course, there are risks to every investment. But the benefits far outweigh the risks in this case.

7 REASONS TO INVEST IN REAL ESTATE

Let's make things easy for you. **Seven solid reasons** why you should invest in real estate. Hopefully, by the end, you'll be convinced—without a doubt—that real estate investing is one of the best financial decisions you can ever make.

Reason 1: Diversify Your Portfolio

Your financial portfolio consists of all your assets and investments you currently own. These include stocks, bonds, cash, and real estate. When your portfolio consists of only one asset, it is called an undiversified or "concentrated" portfolio. You have all your eggs in one basket. For example, if you had gotten in on Amazon early when it first went public in 1997 and paid $18 for five shares, your shares would now be worth $16,477.35 as of March 2022.

Sounds good, doesn't it? But what if that was the only asset you owned in your portfolio? Your wealth is dictated entirely by how Amazon performs, and if Amazon's stock crashed tomorrow, you'd lose everything.

When you diversify your income, you add other assets to your financial portfolio. With a diversified portfolio, you may own some stock in Amazon and some in Starbucks. Perhaps you might add gold investments. Investments in various other areas help offset any losses you might incur if one of your investments goes sideways.

If you invested in Amazon and a few residential homes, even if Amazon's stock tanked suddenly, you would not lose everything because you would still have your real estate assets. It is unlikely that every possible investment will crash at the same time. Real estate provides sturdy security for your financial portfolio—especially if you diversify even further within real estate.

Of course, the downside to diversification is that when your finances are spread wide across various investments, you won't see as much gain if one asset begins to increase. It is part of the risk and reward system of investing. But at least real estate allows you to make your own decisions about your investment.

Reason 2: Control Your Investment

Wherever you decide to invest and put your money, that entity will generally dictate the best use of your money. Even in altruistic investing, the foundation or organization you put money into gets to use that money how they feel is needed (within the parameters you set for them). Even if you own a substantial part of the company in the stock market, there is still much about the company that you cannot decide without jumping through hoops.

Investing in real estate allows you to have complete control of your investment. You can decide who manages your property, how the building is maintained, who gets to rent, and who buys. You can demolish the structure or add to it. Unless you choose to delegate, the choices about that particular property are all dependent on your vision for it.

The amount of time you've held onto a property further decreases the risk of loss. The market dictates the home's value. Holding onto your property and paying off your mortgage means that you will see many ebbs and flows of the market. When the market goes up, your home's value also increases, further building equity. This equity is gold because it allows you to further control your real estate investment by leveraging it to receive a return on your investment.

Reason 3: Potentially Leverage Real Estate

Here is where real estate investors really get to flex their muscles. Leveraging real estate at its most basic is when you borrow from a lender to buy property. Suppose you decide to increase your real estate portfolio. In that case, you'll be using equity—the amount of worth the home has after the mortgage—as the leverage to get a return on your investment. This leverage will allow you to buy more than one property.

Once you've decided on the next property you want to buy, you'll go to a lender and receive a predetermined line of credit based on the equity. You'll use that to pay off whatever mortgage you have left on that home. You can use whatever is left to buy and invest in the new property. Depending on how much you have to invest, you can buy the property in full or make a reasonably sized down payment. As the property value increases, your net worth increases.

Whatever way you use the leverage, the vital thing to note is that you are not using your income streams. The profits gained from your previous investments enable you to leverage your equity and avoid financing through a lender. If you use this method wisely and exercise patience, you will earn a reward of solid investment returns.

Reason 4: Increase Your Tax Benefits

There's a huge benefit to investing in real estate: tax benefits. Your tax benefits have to do with any tax deductions or tax credits earned based on your lifestyle. In this case, we're looking primarily at tax deductions you get to claim due to being a property owner. Less of your income will be subject to tax. This benefit opens a whole gambit of financial moves you can make to maximize your return potential.

The number of tax deductions and their specific effects are vast and depend on the type of property you own and how you use it. You would be wise to speak with a financial advisor about options, especially if you are investing in rental properties.

One of the essential tax deductions for this book is rental property management. You can deduct the cost of owning and managing your investment property at tax time.

Usually, you receive income from the tenants when you have a rental property. You are also simultaneously building equity in the home as it appreciates over time. But you can also deduct any expenses involving insurance, property taxes, travel expenses, and many others.

Another considerable component with tax benefits comes in allowing for depreciation. You'd probably need to speak with a financial advisor on this one, but here are the basics. Instead of taking one significant tax deduction when you buy or improve the rental property, you can alternatively distribute the deduction over the useful life of the property. So, you take more minor deductions every year until you have deducted the property's base value.

The IRS gets pretty picky about using this technique. Again, you should speak with a financial specialist who can help you determine if this is a good move for you and make sure that you meet all the requirements.

Reason 5: Strengthen Your Cash Flow

Here is a straightforward perk. First, you are receiving income from your real estate investment. You can keep the cash available after paying the mortgage and other expenses. This only increases as you pay off the mortgage and build equity in the home.

That's not the only cash flow benefit, however. You can also get tax deductions for cash flow from investment properties. Remember, you can get tax deductions for the operation and maintenance of investment properties. So, as you pay off your mortgage, build equity, and take tax deductions on your investment property, your cash flow only increases over time.

Reason 6: Real Estate Has Physical Value

Unlike stocks and companies, which can plummet and go bankrupt, or cars, which lose value the instant you leave the lot, homes and land will always have value. If the housing market were to drop, your house would still have value and continue to have value whether the housing market rises or falls.

Even if your home value did plummet astronomically low, or if you lost your home in a disaster, that land continues to have value. Investors can even get a tax deduction for property taxes paid on vacant land and other operating expenses.

Reason 7: Real Estate Values "Appreciate"

Along those lines, the final reason most people begin investing in real estate is appreciation. Hundreds of investors have built wealth using various strategies from this one characteristic. Most methods count on a property's ability to appreciate over time.

The property's **appreciation** means the value of the property *rises*. As the property's value rises, investors can make more money through the increased rent or sell the property for more than they bought it for, earning a sizable profit.

Many investors will simply "buy and hold" property for an extended amount of time and then sell or refinance the property when they see that they can make a profit. Although investors can do something similar with stocks, the option for investors to use and hold property to generate income creates more profit-making opportunities.

THE INVESTMENT WAR: REAL ESTATE VS. STOCKS

For years, investors have gone back and forth about the better investment: stocks or real estate. **Stocks** offer a variety of wealth-building opportunities and a more flexible liquidation process. You can pull money much easier and faster from stocks than from real estate.

However, real estate wins the longevity war due to its consistency. While a stock may plummet and never get back to its previous amount, real estate can plummet, but it will inevitably rise again. Property never loses its value. In that way, real estate has less risk than the stock market. However, as in any investment, there are still some risks.

Stocks win the price of investment battle, hands down.

- You decide how many stocks you want to buy from a company and how much you want to spend. You can buy as many or as few as you want and still have an investment. Spending money on buying physical real estate is an "all-in" decision. Making this choice can be unnerving when dealing with five or six-figure numbers.

Diversification and flexibility benefits favor real estate by far.

- While you can mix and match stocks, bonds, and other derivatives, real estate gives you the flexibility of investing in a tangible and controllable asset. You can wield this asset with whatever strategy you want, whether through rentals, buy and hold tactics, or house-flipping. Tangible assets allow for significant diversification in your portfolio.

Finally, there is the time-effort conundrum.

- Most people want to get their money back as quickly as possible with the least effort. If that's the goal, stocks are the way to go.
- Real estate takes time and effort to research and

strategize future action steps.

- Stocks require initial studying but not much else unless you are involved in day trading.
- Real estate takes time to go through the buying process, legal preparations, and other closing details.
- Stocks can be bought and sold with a few clicks.

We could go back and forth for hours (and some people do!) about whether stocks or real estate investing is better. Stocks are usually easier to understand, but real estate really comes alive when you hear about actual people doing it.

Have you ever heard of Josh Altman? He's one of the stars of the show *Million Dollar Listing Los Angeles*. On the show, he's known for closing million-dollar deals on some fantastic luxury listings. Now, most of us will not get to this level of real estate, but what's most important is his story.

Altman began his career in the mailroom of a music management company, sleeping on a couch in a fraternity. But he found that some of the managers were making money on the side by investing in real estate. After doing some research, Josh realized he could flip homes for profit. It wasn't long before he was hooked and continued to grow in the real estate field, eventually making it to the luxury real estate arena.

Believe it or not, his story is not so uncommon. That was my story. I started in a rental of my own, paying money to a landlord who (hopefully) was employing some of the techniques we've mentioned to build his wealth. But I wanted more than to pay for a place to live. I wanted to have my own real estate and invest in others. So, I took a step out and risked investing. I started with one home, then another. Over time, I owned several multifamily homes, which generated passive income and allowed me to be financially secure.

I have over twenty years of hands-on experience, and I've developed a good eye for spotting good deals. You can do the same. So far, we've talked a lot about real estate investment and its pros and cons. But this is not why you're here. This primer was only to get the basics out of the way.

Whether you are a new or seasoned investor, let's focus on the one thing you should get started on—multi-family properties.

3

SMALL STEPS, BIG RETURNS - MULTIFAMILY REAL ESTATE 101

Deciding to invest in properties is one thing; deciding on which to invest in is a different ballgame. This decision-making is where the rubber meets the road. Let's explore and learn more about multifamily real estate and why it's an attractive investment option.

Multifamily real estate describes two categories of properties: The first is Commercial. Apartment complexes, for example, classify under this category. The second is Residential. Homes with less than five units like duplexes or quadplexes are also considered multifamily properties.

We'll primarily look at residential multifamily real estate for our purposes. Still, we also need to understand the history and other forms.

BREAKING DOWN MULTIFAMILY REAL ESTATE

The first multifamily homes were built as apartments before the second world war. These were stately structures with high ceilings and expensive building materials. Many still stand and have survived the test of time. After World War II, more people wanted to live in suburban settings, and the G.I. Bill made that possible for many veterans.

Many homes built after World War II were created with the suburban and single-family format in mind. Large, opulent apartments gave way to shorter, multi-story homes that could hold multiple families. These were more affordable, and many were in communities that provided comfort amenities like pools and parks.

This history is why any residential property with *more than five units where multiple families live* is known as a **commercial multifamily property**. These units must all feature amenities like bathrooms and kitchens to be considered multifamily.

Over time, that term has expanded to include "residential homes" built to accommodate multiple units and which can house more than one family. Homes that share one piece of property, a wall, and split into four (quadplex) or fewer dwellings classify as **residential multifamily homes**.

These homes attract certain kinds of people. Investors (like us) love these sorts of residential homes. They often follow the same lending rules as traditional investment single-family homes. However, they have more significant potential for return on investment since multiple families pay rent. Multigenerational families also like homes like these since they can have each family set in a different house unit. People who live in one unit and rent out all the others get the bonus of using it as a primary residence and profit from the renters' income (a form of "house hacking").

JUST FOR COMPARISON: SINGLE-FAMILY REAL ESTATE

Sometimes people get confused about the difference between single-family homes and residential multifamily properties. This confusion usually happens because of the designation and structure of the homes.

A **single property** with more than one but *less than five livable (including kitchen and bathroom) units* is considered a residential multifamily home. The *multiple units and separate addresses* make it a "multifamily" home. The "less than five units" are what makes it residential.

Single-family homes, in comparison, only have *one livable unit and one address* (even if they have multiple kitchens and bathrooms).

In single and multifamily homes, you can increase the value and potential for appreciation by making improvements and repairs. But in multifamily dwellings, you can also increase your income potential by adjusting rental rates and how many people live in a building.

Single-family home investors must regularly buy homes to increase their income consistently.

THE POWER OF INVESTING IN MULTIFAMILY REAL ESTATE

So, the investment potential of multifamily real estate is what makes it such an attractive option for real estate investors, new and seasoned alike. Many new investors choose to live out of one of the units and rent the rest. This living arrangement is a strategic way to produce passive income through your primary residence without dealing with the added stipulations of secondary and investment properties.

However, there are definite pros and cons to investing in multifamily real estate. One of the main pros is the financial increase in your income. Not only do you receive monthly payments from multiple renters, but you are also entitled to receive tax deductions for home operation and maintenance. As stated before, investing in real estate is also a great way to diversify your portfolio.

Another pro of investing in multifamily homes is the ease of access.

If you choose to live in the home as you're renting out the other properties, you know what's happening in your building and can stop problems long before they become larger ones. Also, it is much easier to handle maintenance issues for multiple tenants in a single location than traveling to numerous single homes with potentially different utility arrangements and setups. Why fix pipes in three other houses for three families when you can repair one line in one home for three families?

But with every pro, there are also cons. One of the biggest cons with multifamily homes is the exertion necessary to run and maintain the property. Indeed, you are not managing multiple houses at once as you would in single-family investments. However, you still have numerous leases, payment arrangements, and other issues you must handle. Even though you can delegate a property management company to deal with those responsibilities, you still must make some decisions as the owner.

Another big con in this arena is the competition for multifamily homes. Depending on where you live, you may struggle to find multifamily homes for affordable prices, if at all. Many people must patiently wait for several months or years for their first chance to invest in a multifamily home, and experienced investors often have the upper hand. Experienced investors can usually pay cash and know what to say and do to make buyers want to sell to them. These advantages put newer investors at a significant disadvantage.

So, especially if you're new to multifamily real estate, what's the point?

5 REASONS TO INVEST IN MULTIFAMILY HOUSING

Let's simplify this again. This time, I'll give you **five solid reasons** why you should invest in multifamily real estate.

Reason 1: Grow Your Real Estate Portfolio and Fast

We talked about the importance of building and diversifying your financial portfolio. Each real estate unit you add further builds and diversifies your real estate portfolio. It is much faster and less work to buy one multifamily property and instantly get four units than buy four individual single-family properties.

Reason 2: Property Management Is an Option

Managing a property can be a huge pain. It requires time and energy that not every investor may enjoy or be able to give. Investors who have two single-family properties may not be able to rationalize that hiring property management makes financial sense. The cost of property management may eat up more of their profits than they are comfortable accepting. However, someone with four units in a multifamily property may be better financially to hire the extra help and save themselves lots of time and effort.

Reason 3: Cash Flow

Creating an increase in cash flow is why you're reading this book. You want financial freedom, and a multi-family home can provide a solid and dependable cash flow. Single-family home investors whose tenants must leave suddenly, for example, are left with a completely vacant property. Therefore, they are no longer receiving any income. However, in a multifamily home, let's say a duplex, if a tenant leaves, you still have at least one other tenant to help offset the costs for that property.

Reason 4: Tax Benefits

As we stated earlier, real estate comes with some great tax benefits. The most significant benefit comes from mortgage interest deduction. In general, the larger the investment property, the higher the mortgage and the higher the interest. These higher numbers mean that multifamily home investors can significantly benefit from a tax deduction at tax time.

Reason 5: Appreciation

While this can apply to single-family homes, you can use it more uniquely with multifamily dwellings. For example, if you choose to live in a unit, you will not have to put as much money down. You can pretty much have anyone who rents from you pay off the mortgage for your home while your building appreciates. Buying and holding for a multifamily home investor allows them to wait through any low home value periods, eventually reaping the rewards of their wait through routine inflation.

SMALL STEPS TO FINANCIAL FREEDOM

So how does investing in multifamily homes get you financial freedom?

First, ask yourself how much you need per month to be **financially secure**. In other words, based on your housing, utilities, food, lifestyle, etc., how much do you spend a month? That's how much you need to be financially secure. To be financially secure, you simply need to have enough for all your monthly expenses, no debt, some savings, and some extra cash. But financial security is not the same thing as financial freedom.

Financial freedom means that you get to have the freedom to live life as you desire. It's the next step up from financial security. Here's a simplified way to think about it: To be financially free, you need to be financially secure—with passive income.

Suppose you have made some traditional investments, such as retirement savings and a few stocks. You also have accumulated your ideal savings and have some liquid cash. You may feel financially secure, but your monthly passive income should equal your monthly expenditures to be financially free. For example, suppose you are financially secure and need $4,000 per month to take care of yourself and your family. You can consider yourself financially free when making $4,000+ in passive income.

Multifamily investing allows you to make that financial freedom number. Let's use the following example:

You buy a duplex for $250,000 and put the standard 20% down, leaving about $200,000 for financing. After all the extra financial figures, your monthly payment for 30 years comes out to $1200. Now let's go ahead and assume that conservative rental comparisons in the area are about $1000 per month for a standard two-bedroom and two bathroom.

Assuming you can fill both those duplex units and charge the rate of $1000/month, that's $2000/month that you are now making. You take that first $1200 and apply it to the mortgage, leaving $800. Assuming you put $400 away for other expenses, you now have $400 in profit. That may seem small, but that is $400/month that you are generating through passive income. That money is just flowing in. You only need ten units to provide that magic financial freedom number.

What happens if you do the same with another duplex? Now that's $800/month. What if you try for a quadplex? Assuming everything scales consistently and you make the same profit, that's $1600/month.

Before you run off and buy your first multifamily property, there is more you need to understand. It would be best to have a clear idea of what you will do once you buy such a property.

4

BEFORE YOU BEGIN INVESTING IN MULTIFAMILY PROPERTIES

The last chapter's information has energized you if you're anything like me. But before you run off to the races to purchase your first multifamily home, there are some things we need to consider first.

REVIEWING THE LANDSCAPE

Before making any investment, you should always know the scope of the landscape. The real estate landscape includes understanding the past trends and the projected shifts.

Historically, multifamily homes have made for very sound investments. Many investors prefer multifamily real estate investments as "defensive investments." Some of this stems from their ability to survive various economic downturns. When the economy drops, multi-family homes tend to produce more income. As economies fail, people lose jobs and may sell homes, opting for rentals with cheaper monthly payments than mortgages and less maintenance. People always need a place to live.

Perhaps it's for this reason that demand for multifamily housing has skyrocketed since the recession of 2008. Since then, multifamily home values have steadily risen as investors compete to find properties that afford them stable passive incomes.

Even more recently, during the 2020 pandemic, multi-family homes remained steady. Despite concerns about people not paying rent due to the high unemployment rates, the opposite was true. Most people continued to keep up their monthly payments, perhaps helped by the multiple stimulus injections from the US treasury.

The challenge is that, as we've climbed out of this economic crisis, home values have begun to increase again. Coupled with the disrupted job market, education, and various other challenges, young adults are less than prepared to buy their own homes. Many young adults opt to live with family or friends. Many more millennials and early Gen Zers are in the market for rentals.

FINANCES AND MANAGEMENT

The landscape may look ideal, but multifamily homes can be expensive. You need to know some basics about financing and managing your investment. Therefore, there are a few things you need to keep in mind before investing in a multifamily home. I will go into some of these concepts later, but here's a general summary for now.

In many cases, financing a multifamily home is more accessible than funding a single-family home. A primary reason is that banks look at multifamily homes as potential multiple-income properties. So, they see them as less risky than single-income properties. They recognize that you'll probably be receiving several incomes from one property. Therefore, you're more likely to get approved for a bank loan.

You also need to be aware of the capitalization rate (cap rate) along the financing lines. The capitalization rate formula may differ slightly among investors, but it is usually something as follows:

Capitalization rate = Net Operating Income/Current Market Value

The capitalization rate is the rate of return on a real estate property based on the income that the property expects to produce. It is essential to be familiar with the cap rate, and we'll spend an entire chapter exploring what it means later. But for now, it's good to note that it helps you measure your return on your investment.

The last thing to keep in mind is property management. You don't have to serve as the landlord or personally manage your property. Multifamily home investors will often hire a property management company. As we saw in previous chapters, hiring a property management company makes financial sense if your income is high enough to accommodate it. A multifamily home generally produces enough income to make this a valid option.

MULTIFAMILY REAL ESTATE TRENDS FOR 2022

The world changes quickly, and it is essential at any stage to be aware of how market and landscape trends are progressing. Analyzing the market trends in 2022 allows us to project and predict where the market is and how multifamily real estate trends may go in the following years.

As we look at the 2020s, we must admit that there have been remarkable and challenging changes in a short amount of time. Housing markets were finally beginning to settle after the housing crisis in 2008. Outlooks were bright before the onset of the coronavirus pandemic.

Despite government intervention and attempts at market correction, the housing market took a hit in more ways than one. The eviction ban placed on homeowners for current tenants created an income vacuum in the pockets of investors. Without the ability to evict tenants who defaulted on rent, as might be the standard way of handling this situation, investors were in a precarious position. Now, they did not have that passive income, nor could they find new tenants to produce income for them to pay the mortgage on their investments. Many investors had to dive into their own pockets to hold on to their current investment properties.

However, there remains a strong demand for these properties. The biggest problem right now is that there is not enough supply. This lack of inventory has caused a battle between investors and first-time buyers trying to break into the real estate market.

We've also seen challenges arise from multifamily homes located in urban areas. While these usually are very well populated, the pandemic and the rising cost of living have begun to move people outside of heavily populated areas and into more suburban and rural areas. Investors in urban and other heavily populated areas are finding that they must put more effort into finding renters for their properties than they may have in the past.

Despite the challenging circumstances currently taking place, the outlook for the real estate market, particularly the multifamily home market, is optimistic.

Millennials currently make up much of the buying force in the United States—many of whom are reaching mid to late adulthood and desiring to build wealth and raise families. However, high-interest rates and job challenges have kept many of them from being able to afford the climbing property prices. Hence, more and more millennials are likely to live in rental properties.

In addition, due to the high inflation rates and low inventory, sellers currently have the pricing power in the market. That will not continue to be the case because, eventually, we will see a drop in the prices of homes as the world begins to resettle and the supply increases. Multifamily dwellings are typically consistent and resilient. Any multifamily home investment continues to have the security of multiple income streams coming from one property. They also continue to appreciate just as they have for many years.

THE 5 KEY STEPS TO MAKING D.E.A.L.S

If you've read to this point, you must be interested in making the life-changing decision to invest in a multi-family property. Doing so can help you generate a passive income that supports you through the thick and thin of any economic impact. Even so, I know you still have some questions:

"But where should I begin? What should be the first step when I want to set out and buy a multifamily home? What should I consider? How do I select the right property? More importantly, how do I know the property's value?"

This process can be daunting. Even if you select the right property, it will take innovative financing to achieve your goals and make it a valuable investment. Once it's yours, you will still need to ensure that it stays in good condition.

I've provided an easy-to-follow system that you can always rely on when you set out to find your first multifamily real estate investment. This method will simplify the process, and it starts with the 5-step process of making **D.E.A.L.S.**

Decision on the Property

The first step you need to take is deciding what kind of multifamily property you want to invest in and what is the best option for your goals. This step involves looking at various factors to pinpoint what the most suitable form of a multifamily property is for you. It also includes finding properties through the proper market channels and assessing multiple factors to ensure what you buy works in your favor.

Examination and Valuation of the Property for Investment

The next step is the valuation of the property you are planning to buy. You must ensure that the location, amenities, and various other factors play in your favor to get the most out of your intended investment. Deciding on your property and evaluating it will be a topic of discussion in the upcoming Part II of this book.

Acquisition of the Property

With the above two points taken care of, this one deals with the "buying" aspect. There are various ways you can buy or finance a multifamily estate, and we will explore all of these in detail in Part III of this book.

Logistics for Sustainability

Finally, it all boils down to running and maintaining your multifamily estate the right way to remain in good condition as a prime asset. We will explore the logistics in detail in Part IV of this book.

Strategies for the Future

Once your property is operational, you can plan for the long run and continue the cycle of investments to generate more capital.

Lots to consider! For years, real estate and its unique benefits have been primarily accessible to the wealthy and connected. But now, those barriers have been removed, and this investment sector is available to everyday people like you and me.

Let's see how the D.E.A.L.S. framework works in aiding you with various aspects of investing in a multifamily property, starting with deciding what you should be buying.

PART - II - DECISIONS AND ASSESSMENTS

5

DECIDING ON YOUR PROPERTY - CRITERIA FOR SELECTION

In Chapter 3, you see the various types of multifamily properties that exist and are available for you as investment options. People often like to think of apartment buildings when considering a multifamily investment. But these aren't the only ones.

When starting in this multifamily home sector, it's often better to stick with the smaller ones. We've mentioned the "-plex" properties before, and these are precisely the kind of multifamily real estate we will be exploring.

The three that we'll be exploring the most for your investments are duplexes, triplexes, and fourplexes (or quadruplexes).

UNDERSTANDING THE "-PLEXES"

Suppose you're investing in duplexes, triplexes, or four-plexes. In that case, you need to understand the characteristics of these multifamily homes and what your tenants will be experiencing. To be considered a duplex, triplex, or fourplex, there need to be multiple individual units all under the same roof and share walls.

A duplex has two units, a triplex has three units, and a fourplex has four units. Anything more than four units would not fall under a -plex configuration. All these buildings are for multiple families.

As we mentioned before, one of the most attractive things about multifamily investments is that you get the benefits of commercial real estate investment without the financing problems. If the property contains under five units, you can still receive a residential home loan for a multifamily property.

People buy these homes for various reasons. Many like to use them for "house hacking" (we'll get more into that later). We've previously listed some of the benefits of small multifamily homes. As a reminder, the smaller multifamily homes allow us to rent out multiple units to multiple people at one time. In addition, they enable us to live in one unit and rent out the others, thereby increasing equity in our home with less cost to ourselves. People also use these homes to have their entire family live in close quarters with them.

Why People Like -plexes

There are many advantages to investing in a -plex property. The first one is that you can set whatever rules you want. The -plex property is a residential property used in much the same manner as a commercial property. So, you can dictate how your tenants should act and what they can and cannot bring into your building. If you're living there, you can keep an eye on your property and ensure that the tenants hold up their end of the lease agreement.

As mentioned before, these properties often qualify for significant tax deductions, making the property more cost-effective. One of these deductions is maintenance, which you can write off during tax season.

Tenants like these buildings because they often have amenities nearby, whether a yard or lawn. They also take up less square footage in a community, meaning that they are ideal for locations where lots of people work. By living in this community, people can live close to work and minimize their commute time.

Why People Dislike -plexes

As with most anything, there is another side to the coin. There are some reasons why people would not like -plex properties.

Privacy is one of the most significant factors. Compared to single-family homes, people who live in -plex properties have less privacy than others. We could probably say the same thing about large apartment complexes. However, there is a general feeling of being part of a large crowd in these buildings, and you end up being a slight drop in a big bucket. Duplex properties offer more intimacy and proximity to others, and not everyone is comfortable with that.

Investing in -plex properties also mean that you have more units to try to keep occupied. Of course, you still receive income if you have even just one unit occupied. However, you're not reaping the full benefit of your investment. In addition, these properties are usually more expensive than single-family homes. So, if you have an outstanding mortgage, the income needed to stay on top of it will probably be more significant.

Duplexes, triplexes, and fourplexes also offer fewer amenities than apartment complexes. There are often pools, gyms, and even golf courses or country clubs in common apartment complexes. Smaller multifamily properties usually do not offer these levels of amenities.

If you choose to house hack and live in one of the property units, you may have issues having your tenant live so close to you. Having this proximity can make you easily accessible. You may have tenants knocking on your door at unwanted times if you haven't set firm boundaries.

On top of that, you still must deal with maintenance and other expenses. Even if you have tenants living on your property, the goal of solely paying off your mortgage is not enough. You may have to pay additional costs, including marketing and landscaping. We'll discuss operating costs more in later chapters.

KNOWING THE CRITERIA

When deciding whether you're going to purchase a -plex property, it's essential to consider all the criteria. Suppose this will be an investment property that produces a certain income level for you, regardless of how large or small. In that case, you must take it seriously and treat it like a business even if you are living there.

You need to look at the purchase price, location, and investment opportunity based on the current demographic in the area. You will also need to consider how much it will cost to screen tenants or any other processes you want to put in place for your rental property. All of these are additional expenses.

For example, say you determine that you want to hire a lawyer to draw up a simple lease for you to ensure that it is law binding and sound—that is an extra expense. If you would like to screen tenants and require background checks or credit checks, that is also an additional expense. Hiring a real estate professional to speak with you and to look at market analysis and options in the area could be more money.

These are essential considerations and expenses that you must give due diligence before handing over any money for that property. After you determine all your needs and ensure this is a property that makes financial sense for you, you will need to meet with several lenders before purchasing a property.

Location, Location, Location

It's an often heard saying in real estate that location is everything. And it's so common because it's true. One of the most significant decisions you can make for your property is where it will be. Pick the wrong spot, and you may end up not having a single person who wants to live there or charging meager rent to incentivize people to come to your property. Ideally, you find a balance between having the right people and setting the right amount.

One thing to keep in mind is the amenities in the surrounding area. These can include anything from local supermarkets to schools and school districts. The right amenities in the right location can help draw the right people. You will also want to see how well developed and how successful the local area is. For example, universities in the area that are not producing quality students may not attract a quality level of a tenant. If you have a property next to a notorious entity known as a "party school," you may attract tenants who could potentially damage or not care for your property.

If you live in an area with young professionals or business owners, you may find the local real estate attracts people willing to pay a premium because they want to be close to their place of work.

Knowing the average pay in the area will also be helpful. For example, do you live where people have a high economic status? Are people able to pay the level of rent that you were hoping to charge?

Population and Demographics

Population and demographics can play a prominent role in whether people want to buy or live on your property. Anyone who begins living in a new area wants to know that they can feel safe and secure in that community. Home values and development reflect this fact.

People also tend to move wherever jobs are. So, if you are in an area with positive job growth, you can expect to have an influx of people and thus more opportunities for tenants. In addition, you would also want to make sure that the household income reflects the population of people that you will be able to afford with your pricing.

Crime is also a significant factor when it comes to population demographics. Although clearly, not everyone in a particular neighborhood is a criminal, high-crime areas can reflect the culture of the environment in that area. Historically, there's a correlation between crime rates in a community and the number of tenants who frequently default on rent.

Many websites provide accessible recent crime statistics, and of course, you'll want to look at the local sex offender registry. However, it would also be helpful for you to go and explore the area yourself. Nothing beats getting a personal view of the property you are considering purchasing.

The number of homes currently being built or renovated is significant to note as you tour the neighborhood. These usually indicate a growing market. You can also grasp the population demographics of the area by looking at the retail stores nearby. Expensive stores would not waste money building in areas where they know people would not be able to afford their products.

REAL ESTATE PROPERTY TYPES

There are many diverse types of real estate that classify as multifamily real estate assets. Most multifamily properties can be classified A–D, and let's look at some of these classifications.

Class A

Class A properties were usually built within the last ten years and mainly comprised of top-class luxury properties. These may come with several luxury amenities (pools, tennis courts, etc.) and are usually in high-income areas. The luxury lifestyle is also reflected in the price since these tend to be the most expensive properties.

Class B

Class B properties were usually built within fifteen to twenty years. These are still luxury properties and have traditionally been well-maintained. Most investors typically purchase these for appreciation rather than the cash flow.

Class C

Class C properties have usually been built over thirty years ago. They are often outdated and may require funds to update or repair different aspects of the property. Many investors choose to profit from this type of property by taking advantage of the state of disrepair and adding value to the home through renovations and repairs. These are usually sources of good cash flow for multifamily home investors. They often attract renters who desire to live there because they can't afford more expensive rents or mortgages.

Class D

Class D properties were usually built over forty years ago. They are generally run-down and not well kept, and they may be in very low-income or high-crime neighborhoods. Often property management in these properties is a challenge.

LET'S TRY SOME PRACTICE

We've spent this chapter exploring ways to decide on your property. Let's practice some essential investigation. Go to any property website (realtor.com, zillow.com, etc.) and filter for "multifamily homes" only. See what the website shows you for your area.

Investigate the property. Check out the year of construction, how many units it offers, and the property's condition. You may even try to "type class" it as A–D.

Once you have a shortlist of multifamily properties, put the address into Google Maps and look at some of the businesses and community properties surrounding it. Are there schools and parks nearby? What about professional companies or supermarkets?

Get some practice doing this with multiple properties. As I mentioned before, nothing can take the place of personal, hands-on exploration. But looking up properties online is an excellent first step.

As we move to this next chapter, I want to mention one important factor worth considering: a concept to understand in real estate—the capitalization rate. Let's explore this further.

6

CAPITALIZATION RATE 101

I know, I know. This chapter might feel like a break in searching for the right multifamily property, but it's important and can't be left behind. It's a factor that you will utilize when evaluating the property. After all, it is THE most crucial metric in real estate—so it's better to gain clarity on it once and for all.

CAPITALIZATION RATE - THE BASICS

In a nutshell, the capitalization rate (cap rate) is used by investors to determine the profit or loss generated by an investment over time. There are many ways to calculate this rate; however, this is the most common:

Cap Rate = Net Operating Income/Market Value of Asset

You would subtract your operating and management expenses from the property's gross income to determine the net operating income.

Your **operating expenses** include property tax, insurance, repairs, management, etc. Note: This number does *not* include the mortgage, and the mortgage is not considered an operating expense. Excluding debt allows investors to focus on the property income alone.

Your gross income (also called total revenue) includes any rent or other income sources on the property, such as vending machines or coin-operated laundry rooms.

The market value of the property is dependent on investor valuations. This value indicates how much the property is worth. This number can be dynamic, rising and falling with the housing market. Any repairs or renovations that you complete will also influence the property's value. Many investors may have to ask a professional appraiser to provide a valuation.

So, what does the cap rate look like in practice? Let's go back to our $250,000 duplex from Chapter 3. If you remember, we currently receive $1,000 per unit per month. That is $2,000 per month. After expenses (*don't include mortgage!*), you are left with $1600 per month in profit. That totals to $19,200 per year. We'll also assume that the $250,000 home value remains consistent. Let's put that into our equation.

$19,200 (NOI)/$250,000 (market value) = 7.7%

What do you think? Is the capitalization rate lower or higher than you'd like? Does it work for you?

The insight here is why the capitalization rate is so important to know. Using this equation, you can determine if a property is worth the price, how much you would need to charge for rent, and if the property is a sound investment.

Many multifamily investors usually feel that a cap rate around 4% - 10% is sound. It looks like we've got a decent property here so far!

MULTIFAMILY INVESTMENT

Cap rates can apply to all property assets, but multifamily investments have a few extra considerations. Some of these considerations have to do with its lower investment risk. Cap rates can be considered a risk measurement.

Low cap rates in an area usually indicate that properties have a high value. Having a low cap rate is perceived as less risky because the area is well developed, and property values are holding or growing.

Higher cap rates in an area usually indicate there may not be much growth or influx of businesses and professionals. Since the properties may not have high value or fluctuate, property owners rely on higher net operating incomes to compensate, which means higher cap rates.

This analysis becomes essential when looking at multifamily properties because they tend to have lower average cap rates than other properties. But even with multifamily properties, cap rates can shift dramatically.

One of the most significant influences on cap rates is the location. Larger cities tend to have lower cap rates because of their high population concentration and increased property values. Smaller towns have higher cap rates because the property values are likely to fluctuate and have a greater vacancy risk due to the lower population concentration.

Property type, which we described in the last chapter, also plays a significant role. Newly built properties are more likely to hold their value, while old properties are more at risk of losing their value.

HOW TO WIELD THE CAP RATE

Now that you understand the cap rate better, let's discuss how to use it.

Cap rates begin to shine when you use them as comparison data for other properties in the area. By comparing the cap rate of your property to the cap rates of different properties, you can glean whether you will be profitable from your next financial move.

There are two main reasons people look at the capitalization rate.

The first reason is to know if a property under consideration is worth purchasing and whether the price is reasonable. The second reason is to learn a property's value to know how to price it when selling.

Using Cap Rate to Sell

Let's look at selling first. Perhaps you are considering selling your duplex property from Chapter 3. You already know that your net operating income is $19,200. So, you look at similar duplex properties in the area that have sold within the last five months. You find four properties that are very similar to yours. They are also duplexes with minimal amenities and the appropriate property size.

Working with a real estate agent (ideally the one you plan to list with), you determine that the average cap rate for these four properties is 6.1%. To determine your selling price, you can use the following formula:

Net Operating Income/Cap Rate = Sale Price

So, in this case, you would calculate:

$$\$19,200/.061 = \$314,754$$

So, the approximate value of your property would be around $314,754. Once you have that number, you can set the asking price of your property.

Using Cap Rate to Buy

To use the cap rate to buy an investment property, you would get information about the prospective properties' net operating income and expense details. Examining the individual expenses and revenue streams is essential because you might notice a business flaw in the current model. You may find you can cut costs or increase revenue somewhere.

After you have the net operating income, you can do the same thing you did when selling. You take four properties and get an average sold cap rate.

Let's say that you are buying a new property in the same area as your last property. The asking price is $350,000, and the cap rate is the same, 6.1%. Let's also say that the net operating income from this particular property is $20,500. So, you do your formula:

$$\$20,500/.061 = \$336,065.57$$

Is this an ideal price for you? Although it is ~$14,000 over the asking price, could other factors explain a higher asking price? If not, the property may not be worth the investment as is. If you see a higher net operating income potential after making some changes, you can account for that. Input your projected net operating income and see if that changes the value.

Let's say that you noticed you could increase the NOI by $2,000. So, the NOI would be $22,500. You input that into your calculations:

$$\$22,500/.061 = \$368,852.46$$

Now the projected value is over the asking price! You could be getting an undervalued property due to an inefficient business model.

Calculating the cap rate is essential when searching and deciding on a solid investment property. However, many factors outside of the cap rate indicate whether a property is a good investment or not.

BEWARE OF THESE ISSUES

Cap rate is a tool, and, like any tool, you must use it in its correct form to effectively do its job. A good understanding of cap rate requires us also to explore the problems that often arise when using it as a single indicator of property value.

One of the main issues with cap rate is that it can't account for every potential change in and around a property. Cap rate doesn't account for dramatic economic shifts (e.g., the 2008 crisis or the COVID-19 pandemic), unexpected repairs or construction needs, or fluctuating vacancy rates.

Buyers and sellers can also fudge, muddle, or exaggerate cap rates. Each party wants to paint the cap rate in the best possible light for the best possible deal. Cap rates also don't account for outstanding debts that may roll over to the new owner when purchasing the property. A fundamental rule of thumb for cap rate is to use it as a baseline measurement.

Cap rates can also be a great way to convey to others the type of property you are looking to purchase. By stating that you want something around a 5% cap, brokers and other professionals will know that you are hoping to find something where you can repair or renovate the property.

You'll also want to compare the loan constant to the cap rate. If the cap rate indicates your rate of return, the loan constant indicates your loss rate due to debt. The loan constant measures the percentage of money paid each year to service a debt compared to the total value of the loan itself.

Let's go back to our Chapter 3 duplex one last time. We established that you pulled out a $200,000 mortgage (debt) to buy the duplex. After interest, your payment per month would be $1200 per month. Annually that comes to $14,400. So, your loan constant would be:

$$\$14,400/\$200,000 = 7.2\%$$

So, your loan constant is 7.2%. Assuming your cap rate is the same as the first time we did it, the cap rate should be 7.7%.

In this case, the cap rate is greater than the loan constant, which is good. Although the difference isn't much, we should still be getting a return on our property. When the loan constant exceeds the cap rate, the loan hurts the returns. Even in this case, it would be best to investigate your investment thoroughly to ensure adequate returns.

Remember, cap rates are applicable as an analysis tool but should never be the deciding factor for whether to invest in a property.

PRACTICE CALCULATING CAP RATE

If you'd like more practice with cap rate calculations, here are some examples you can use to sharpen your skills:

You're interested in a triplex property that costs $400,000. Your desired cap rate is above 7%. After speaking with the current owners and investigating, you can determine that the net operating income is about $20,000 per year. Calculating for cap rate, will this property meet your target cap rate?

You are finally ready to sell a quadplex you've had for several years. Market prices have changed since you bought the property. After talking to brokers and doing research, you've determined that the average cap rate of similar properties is now 8%. Your annual net operating expenses are about $15,000, and your current income is $4800 per month. What is a fair price to put on your property?

You can find answers at the end of the book.

That's a lot of math! But understanding the capitalization rate is essential for helping you make quality investment decisions. With all that taken care of, let's see where you can find a suitable property to purchase.

7

THE SEARCH FOR YOUR PROPERTY

We're back! After that detour to explore capitalization, we can now return to deciding on a property. Searching for a property is not difficult, and they usually show up in most cities. However, locating them can be challenging, especially if you don't have access to the same resources as other real estate investors.

HOW TO FIND YOUR MULTIFAMILY PROPERTY

Online forums, networking, and joining different real estate social groups can give you leads on who to talk to or upcoming properties for sale. But most people only have two options: You can either find someone to help you search for your property or go about it yourself.

Do It Yourself

There are many reasons to search for and buy your multifamily property on your own. One of the most obvious is the cost. If you are taking care of the buying process, the seller doesn't have to pay a commission to a broker or agent to help sell the property. You can sometimes negotiate that money be taken off the selling price since that can be factored into the price point.

If you are interested in searching and undergoing the negotiation process yourself, you'll have to do some leg work. Most people don't want to put in the time and effort, so they hire real estate professionals to do the work for them. But if you are willing, you'll want to keep an eye on all the typical real estate websites like realtor.com and zillow.com.

You may also want to check out local auctions and websites with foreclosures. The buying process is slightly different for these but still relevant to the search. You may also want to join a **real estate investment association (REIA)**. You can get good leads and connect with people looking to buy and sell properties.

Often, you can browse options of available rentals in the area you'd like to invest. Sometimes you can find pictures of run-down or non-updated places, which may indicate an owner who cannot afford repairs or renovation. Even better, someone ready to sell and get the property off their hands.

Make sure to take advantage of digital resources like applications for Trulia and Zillow. Often, they have an alarm function that will send new postings that meet your criteria straight to your phone or email.

Driving around neighborhoods and scouting homes that don't look well-kept or updated is another hands-on way of finding potential investment properties. Looking at old ads for rental properties can also be helpful in your fact-finding mission. Sometimes owners are tired of finding, screening, and renting to tenants, and they may be looking to sell and relieve themselves of that work.

Getting Help from Someone

There is nothing wrong with asking for some help in this process, especially if you are just dipping your toe into the multifamily investment arena.

When asking for help, check with the company to see which agents usually deal in multifamily units or have experience working with investors. They will often know where the best deals and areas are in your budget. They also have access to the **multiple listing service (MLS)**, which contains listings of all known properties for sale in a given region.

If you're getting help to buy a home, keep in mind that the commission cost is usually included in the home's sales price. Most people expect buyers to be working with agents and plan accordingly. Commissions are generally 3–7% of the sales price, but they don't come directly out of your pocket.

If investing in multiple properties is part of your long-term plan, building a relationship with a realtor can be helpful. Since they know you are on the lookout for numerous investments, they may be willing to communicate with you quickly as new properties arise in the market. Sometimes, they may even give you a lead before it hits the market.

SEARCHING ON-MARKET

There are many places you can look to find new properties, and some take more leg work than others. There are properties available both on-market and off-market. Depending on where you find your prospective property, you may discover fiercer competition as multifamily homes become more popular investments.

You'll find properties listed by agents or brokers if you search on-market. These people sell the homes for the seller and do all the legwork for the buying process. If you are a seller, these professionals are invaluable. They can help find and negotiate deals and settle on a closing agreement. Sometimes they can be expensive, and you will need to communicate thoroughly. If they send you something you like and wish to explore further, share why you want that characteristic or characteristics.

The Multiple Listing Service (MLS)

The MLS is an optimal place to start when dealing with on-market properties. While many realtors have their own MLS process, many commercial MLS options are available for your use. If sellers list their property on an MLS, they have already gone through valuing and committing to an ideal price range.

Standard MLS services include LoopNet, CREXi, Apartmentbuildings.com, and Showcase. There are many more, and a simple search will often yield a solid list of MLS options for inquiries. All the ones listed and many others include filters that allow you to specify the type and the price point of the property you are trying to find.

SEARCHING OFF-MARKET

If you are searching off-market, things change quite a bit.

Off-market deals are how the *real* deals get done for many more seasoned investors. Many of the best deals never show up on the market because investors who have been networking for years have already scooped them up. Usually, they are thrown the lead early by brokers or other investors they know. Consider partnering with a seasoned investor who can show you the ropes.

If you're searching off-market, you are working on your own to dig up leads and find properties. Usually, this involves contacting the property owner of the home you would like to see and inquiring whether they are looking or willing to sell. Even if they are not ready, hold onto their information so you can reach out to them later when they might be more interested. One great strategy is to look for apartments that are advertising rental space. If a unit is vacant, then the owner is losing money. An apartment advertised as a rental space is a scenario where it might be an ideal time to share with the owner your name and your willingness to purchase their property.

Along with contacting property owners, consider reaching out to commercial and multifamily home brokers. You can find their names on MLS websites, ads for homes, or just by searching online. Reach out to them and introduce yourself. Convey to them that while you aren't interested in what they currently have, you'd like to know if they come across the investment-type properties you seek. Make sure you plan out what you want to say to them. You may not get much from the first conversation, but you may finally get a broker willing to give you a deal after fifty calls.

Along the lines of networking, some other unusual contacts you may want to make include estate attorneys, builders, and wholesalers.

Estate attorneys deal with the management of estates —often dealing with creditors or other issues. Most are willing to work with an investor if it means less work.

Builders are a great source of information because they will often talk about other projects they've worked on recently or plans for other projects. They can also provide insight on jobs where investors begin but couldn't finish developing the home. Suppose you're interested in value-add properties or buying a home for cheap and completing a renovation. In that case, they can give you great leads.

Wholesalers are intermediaries. They buy the contract for a property and then assign or sell it to a prospective investor. They're great sources of investment deals, but you may not get as great a deal as if you went to the seller yourself.

ADDITIONAL RESOURCES

These are a couple of additional resources to keep in mind as you search for the ideal property. Many more websites can provide information about properties, brokers, and sales data.

CoStar.com - provides detailed information on commercial real estate, including news, property information, and public record data.

Mashvisor.com - collects listing information and provides investment opportunities in your area of interest and projections on returns of those properties. This site also provides a heat map analysis that identifies some of the top-performing properties in a given area.

THE 1% RULE

We'll go into more detail about the 1% rule in the next chapter, but it does relate to your search for the ideal property.

The 1% rule states that *a good investment with positive cash flow will be any property whose monthly rent is equal to or greater than 1% of the purchase price.*

For example, if a property generates $1,000 per month of rent, then we follow the formula:

$$\$1,000/.01 = \$100,000$$

Based on this formula, the ideal property value should be $100,000.

This method is neither scientifically nor economically sound. Still, it does help to provide a snap perspective of what could make for a decent investment. It is not a hard and fast rule. When we look at cap rates, so many other factors come into play when making a sound, quality investment decision.

We can also use the 1% rule to decide what rent should be. For example, let's say you have a quadruplex with a market value of $500,000. When trying to determine a baseline for rent, you can use the following formula:

$$\$500,000 \text{ x } .01 = \$5,000$$

So, the total monthly rental income should be at least $5,000 to have a positive cash flow for this property.

The most significant benefit to the 1% rule is that it allows investors to decide quickly whether a property is worth examining further. If an investor is looking at several properties, they may focus on only those who pass the 1% rule.

The biggest downside to this rule is that it doesn't consider anything else. A property can still be an excellent investment, even if it doesn't pass the 1% rule. For example, if operating expenses are low, the net operating income may be higher than expected. The owner may not be charging an appropriately determined rent for leased apartments.

There are several other real estate calculations to know, and we'll explore them more in the next chapter. One such calculation is the 50% rule. This rule states that operating expenses (other than mortgage) should be half the gross rental income. Again, this is not a completely stable rule, and it has deficits. Still, it helps provide a general picture of good investment opportunities.

The **gross rent multiplier (GRM)** helps determine how long it will take to pay off a property based on the rent and its purchase price. It is determined by dividing the purchase price by the gross annual rent. The lower the number, the more profitable your investment property may be.

These are just a few calculations to determine if your prospective property is ideal. Once you've found some properties you deem suitable, it is time to evaluate them and decide whether they are worth your investment.

8

PROPERTY ANALYSIS 101 – EXAMINATION, VALUATION, AND PROFITABILITY ASSESSMENT

S o, you found this sweet-looking multifamily property that *looks* pretty good and is relatively cheap. You feel that you will be able to get good returns on it. So, you decide to go ahead and finalize the deal.

Except you shouldn't. Not yet, at least. There are still many things that you need to consider before finalizing a property—multifamily or not—especially when you want to buy it for investment purposes.

Without knowing what a property is genuinely worth, making any form of investment can be disastrous, especially to the capital you put forward to secure the deal. Once you start "working" the place, you could soon find out that the promises were a lie, and now your investment sits like a heavyweight on your shoulders.

Before you take any purchasing or financing step, always analyze, and evaluate your selection of properties. You will need to assess and consider many factors, including location, investment opportunity, profit, cash flow, and overall valuations.

HOW MUCH POTENTIAL IS IN THIS PROPERTY?

Determining the potential in a property is a crucial skill when doing your initial analysis. You want to have the ability to discern just how much you can get out of the property.

Location and the look of a rental can help increase the appreciation of any property. Suppose you buy a property in a poor area. In that case, it carries minimal potential because it will not appreciate at a fast rate, if at all. In addition, you may also suffer additional damages to your property from crime and poor tenant care.

Speaking of the care for your property, you will also want to make sure that you are aware of any current damages or distressed conditions of your property. Sometimes, to get a better deal, you may have to go with a foreclosure or a property that is still being renovated or completed. In these cases, you'll want to analyze the costs of repairing or building the property. Often this cost can outweigh the benefits.

A thorough evaluation of a property may seem like a tall order, and in a way, it is. You should heavily consider employing help to ensure you do not miss anything. Unless you are a professional contractor or inspector yourself, it's better to get a professional opinion. Sometimes, builders may not construct dwellings correctly and, in other instances, might be structurally sound but not built to code.

These issues can cause significant problems for property owners in the long run. When working with an inspector, make sure that you receive a property report that can give you a comprehensive view of the property's condition. This knowledge will provide you with a critical negotiating point for that property. You may find yourself able to get a better deal and increase the profit potential of your property.

Another critical step in assessing and evaluating the potential of a property is to look at its current financial situation. This analysis includes outstanding debt, reconciled debt, property investments, repairs, and operating expenses. Current rental income, and anything else that involves the property's financial condition, both past and present, should be included.

This financial information is sometimes called a **real estate pro forma**.

By looking at these economic data points, you may see ways to improve upon the current financial situation and whether that is something you want to do when investing in your property.

THE PROFIT POTENTIAL ASSESSMENT

Once you determine that this property has the potential for a return on your investment, it's time to determine whether the profit potential is worth your time and effort. Often you may see properties that have a good return on investment, but after further assessment, you notice that other properties in the area have a greater return.

When assessing profit potential, you will always start with the purchase price. At what cost is the seller listing the property? Compare this to other properties with similar characteristics. If you were looking at a duplex, look at different duplexes with similar square footage in the area. If you were looking at a triplex, look at other triplexes with similar amenities built around the same year or have the same level of renovation. Make a note of the average cost of these properties.

Next, look at the overall cost of that property. Looking at the purchase price is just your starting point. It would help if you now started factoring in the cost of repairs and the overall closing costs. These are usually not included in the listed asking price. The closing costs include attorney fees, application fees, and taxes.

You will also need enough cash for the down payment. If this total is outside your current budget, you may want to rethink the property. You'll also want to determine how much income the property can produce. The seller should include this in the pro forma and any revenue generated by laundry facilities and vending machines.

You'll want to pay close attention to the property's net operating income. Remember the equation for Net Operating Income (NOI):

Net Operating Income = Gross Income of Property - Operating Expenses

The net operating income is crucial to deciding whether this property is worth your time and if it will be of any profit to you. It's also vital in helping you determine what your cash flow is. Your cash flow is simply your net operating income with the mortgage payment subtracted. Mortgage payments often include taxes and homeowners insurance.

Cash Flow = Net Operating Income - Mortgage Payment

This number is based entirely on what you as an investor want. If you are hoping to achieve financial freedom solely with this property, you will want to make sure that your return on investment can help you reach that goal. To determine the percent of return on investment, you will divide the total return by the investment costs.

Return on Investment (ROI) = (Initial Value - Final Value)/Cost of Investment

That number gives you your total return on investment. Remember that this does not account for the value of appreciation of your property. However, it gives you a base idea of how much you should be seeing come back to you after investing in this property. This computation is another way to assess profitability.

GIVING YOUR PROPERTY A VALUE

To effectively evaluate your multifamily property, you'll need to apply all the concepts we've learned in the last few chapters. The first thing to do is conduct the proper market research. Make sure you carefully evaluate the neighborhood. Look up comparables in the area and analyze the price offered for them or the price they last sold. Compare that to the price point requested for your current property.

As we discussed earlier, evaluation of your repairs and determining how to handle those repairs are essential in the decision-making process.

Are you going to perform the repairs yourself? Are you hiring a professional to come in and make the repairs? Consider this when evaluating costs. In Chapter 6 and this chapter, we've talked about the net operating income. You must know how much you should expect to receive from your property.

You'll tie all this together to give your property value. We talked about the cap rate in Chapter 6. We'll also use that method to assign a value to the property. Remember, this value is not a hard and fast rule. But it will help us to determine the value we should be paying for the home.

THE 50% RULE

We mentioned the importance of the 50% rule in the last chapter, and we'll continue to build on that here.

The 50% rule is a valuable tool that allows investors to understand the operating expenses that their rental property will produce. All you do is multiply the property's rental income by 50%. The rental income does not include mortgage, taxes, or depreciation values. You can also apply the 50% rule to each unit within a multi-family home.

Often operating expenses can be hard to predict until you get a detailed form or pro forma from the current owner. In some cases, the property may have never been rented, or there may be shifts or changes unaccounted for when you purchased the property. Whatever the case, you can often determine initial operating expenses in a general way from the 50% rule formula.

This formula is perfect for determining your cash flow by subtracting the rental income's mortgage payment and total operating expenses.

Net Rental Income - Mortgage Payment - Operating Expenses = Cash Flow

Although a valuable tool in the short term, the 50% rule has a few downsides. Of course, the number one downside is that it cannot accurately predict your property's exact operating expense number. You will not know that until you have received a pro forma or have been able to perform your expense analysis on the property. This lack of certainty means that you can underestimate the cost of operating expenses or overestimate them.

The operating expenses may be far less in some cases if you make minor changes to the current model. You might find that although the 50% rule gives you a ball-park number, you were able to cut costs in certain places to find a much lower operating expense number.

But keep in mind, the 50% rule is a fast rule. When you have many properties sitting in front of you, this tool can help you weed them out quickly. This estimate allows us to determine if a deal may even be worth looking at in more detail. All that remains is for you to perform the due diligence.

9

DUE DILIGENCE MATTERS

When we talk about performing due diligence in real estate, we are talking about making sure you know everything about your property. Due diligence primarily means understanding the risks you incur by buying and operating out of this property.

To help you with your due diligence, the guidance in this chapter will guide you to find places that other people might miss. We'll also discuss some of the most common problems property owners find when purchasing a property and how to make sure that you are asking the right questions along the way.

WHAT IS DUE DILIGENCE?

In real estate, due diligence often means that we understand the facts about the property that we're buying. That includes the physical, financial, and legal. We're doing our homework, crossing the t's, dotting the i's, and checking our results.

When dealing with real estate, primarily residential real estate, we often see a certain amount of time built into the contract process. Once you negotiate a deal and the contract process is underway, time is allotted for potential buyers to ask the right questions, investigate, and discern the overall state of the property. Typically, these periods last about 10 to 15 days. However, more or less time can be negotiated with the seller as part of the terms. It's important to note that the less time you have in your due diligence period, the less that you may be able to catch.

Your research shouldn't only happen when the contract period starts; it should happen all along the way. Before submitting an offer on your property, you should analyze everything we've discussed in the past few chapters.

You should include any financial information you can get your hands on during this precontract check. You don't want to enter a due diligence period without knowing how the money comes and goes. Having only ten days to conduct the assessment and sitting at a table trying to sort through stacks of financial information is inefficient.

You can often get a lot of this information beforehand, usually through public records or the seller. Asking for a pro forma is an excellent first step to getting some of that initial financial information. Remember to make sure the financial details include:

- gross rental income repairs
- maintenance property taxes
- insurance
- any other debt or loss of revenue due to vacancy and credit

Once you make an offer, due diligence evolves into something slightly different. Now you're on the clock, and this is when you can do your official inspections. Make sure that your assessments include all details about the condition of each room of the property. Check for lead-based paint, verify any flood zones, and examine the utility and mechanical systems like plumbing, electrical, and HVAC.

You should now have the ability to fully access all financial information you'll need for this period. This information includes a long list of items, some of which would consist of:

- current rent rolls
- allowance for pets and pet rent
- lease terms and agreements
- service contracts with different businesses (think landscaping and property management)
- access to the previous owner's property income tax

Now is also the time to check into any legal issues or rights awareness. You are well within your rights as a prospective homebuyer to ask for any information on legal or loan matters that the house has undergone in the last few years. This information includes the cost of title insurance, any pending litigation filed against the property, or any organization connected to the property.

Ask about extra fees from the county, HOA, or other managing bodies. The seller should also be sharing all information about the home that needs addressing. They are legally obligated to do so. These are usually disclosures regarding any material defects in the structure of the building and any information about the previous treatment of rodents or wood-destroying insects.

Feel free to question the seller on any aspect of the property. If there is something you feel the seller should remedy before you buy the property, you can have them do so. If they refuse, you have the right to withdraw the contract.

This period is precisely what due diligence is for— making sure that everything is in order before they hand you the keys and you hand them the money.

CONDUCTING THE GRAND EVALUATION

Your due diligence includes the most crucial evaluation you will make for your property. Since you're looking at this property for investment purposes, your assessment needs to encompass anything that could be a safety hazard or reflect poorly on you as a rental property owner.

We've talked a lot about different things to pay attention to, but this is where we can break down all those factors into one grand evaluation. Ideally, you should divide your due diligence into three main areas: physical property, financial status, and legal standing.

Physical Property

When examining the property, you'll need to make a condition assessment and perform walkthroughs of every unit in the building. A thorough vetting gives you an overall picture of the state of your property. It would be best to invite the inspectors to check out the property during this period. These inspectors should include your home inspection, utility inspection, and rodent and pest inspection.

In addition to these overall inspections, you'll want to conduct your own assessment. Try viewing your property as though you were a tenant. Take time to walk the grounds, climb stairs (if there are stairs), look out the windows and see what the view is, drive as if you were going to park in a parking spot nearby, and pull out of the parking space as if you were going to work.

As part of the physical evaluation, you may also want to spend some time in any property's public spaces. That can include gardens, front porches, or even benches across the street. These are common living areas that your potential tenants may also utilize. You want to make sure that there is no concern for discomfort or safety.

To that end, take an overnight drive on the street. Evaluate the lighting on the road and determine if you need any additional lighting at the front of your property. Factors like these can impact safety and make a property less desirable to tenants. Pay attention to any exposed wiring or rusted pipes. These can be indicative of more significant problems. You will also want to note where any electrical panels or water valves are. In an emergency or a crisis with utilities, you must know these positions.

Always remember you can negotiate any deficiencies in your property with the seller. Make sure that you are meticulous in your evaluation. Don't skip any areas. After you've got an idea of the potential needs of the property, it's time to look at how those can weigh in on the next portion of your evaluation.

Financial Status

This next part of your evaluation is the financial status and potentially the most important one. First, it's good to begin with the physical assessment to note any repairs which could affect your negotiation with the seller. You must consider everything about the property to determine whether the purchase makes financial sense.

You should ideally complete market analysis well before due diligence. However, it is not uncommon for market analysis to occur during the due diligence process (see Chapters 6, 7, and 8). You can do some of it while driving around and learning more about the surrounding communities. While doing a market analysis, you need to ensure that you are looking at your direct competition.

Compare the rental rates and the overall purchase prices of two properties with the same characteristics in your area. Evaluate the demographic data to see the population of people more likely to be attracted to these properties based on the region. Inspect the overall appearance of the property—if it's clean or has new or old fixtures, etc.

Also, inspect how the current owner handles utilities at the property. Are they bundled into the overall rent and paid through the owner? Or are they left to the responsibility of the tenants?

During this evaluation, it's wise to begin building a budget. You can start this task by creating your pro forma or requesting the pro forma of the seller. You should also be requesting any financial data regarding how the property has performed over the last few years. It is essential to look at the history of the property value and rent to see if it fits your rate of return and your ideal capitalization rate.

It is also an excellent opportunity to look for any revenue growth potential during this time. Is the current owner taking full advantage of the resources at their disposal? Are there places where you can install vending machines or laundry facilities that can help increase revenue? Is the rent indicative of the quality of the apartment, or does it leave room to be raised?

Lastly, review the market volatility in the area. Ensure that there is a market for your property and that it will continue to appreciate based on previous and projected data. You can achieve this by looking at the historical information for other properties in the area and requesting any historical financial data for your particular property.

Legal Standing

Many different components fall under legal standing. It can encompass insurance claims, lawsuits against the building, or other outside legal issues. Other legal factors might include making sure you have attorney's fees sorted out and the lease process for future tenants is sound. Ultimately, the property contract between you and the seller should reflect your arrangement with them.

Also included in the legal standing are any arrangements made with outside parties, including landscaping services, security services, cleaning services, and property management services. You should have copies of all contracts for any utilities and warranty documents and environmental reports or engineering evaluations.

Ensuring your property is up to code will help mitigate any legal claims from tenants if they endure property damages or injuries during their stay with you. If you or the seller are unsure, you can always contact the city to find previous inspections on that particular property over the past few years.

Note any liens, poor titles, or an invalid certificate of occupancy. If the certificate of occupancy is incorrect, it can cost you thousands of dollars to remedy. A certificate of occupancy can become null when someone takes liberties to describe a property as something it is not. For example, if someone were to call a duplex a triplex and try to say that it has more units than it does, it would be invalid.

THE MULTIFAMILY HOME CHECKLIST

I have compiled a non-exhaustive list of common (and uncommon) things you should keep in mind. Use this as a basis for formulating your evaluation when you're ready.

Physical Property

- Inspect the entire property (including individual units).
- Night walk/drive around the area.
- Request disclosure of any repairs or dated standards (outlets not grounded, lead-based paint, etc.).
- Request for Environmental Site Assessments, Audits, and Reports.
- Document any amenities and community assets nearby (schools, parks, etc.).
- Make a note of any services like laundry, internet, etc.
- Take photographs of the property and request any recent pictures taken of the property.
- Make a note of any energy-efficient (green) appliances, electronics, or structures.

Financial Status

- Request a financial audit report.
- Perform a local market analysis.
- Obtain a rent roll for all tenants.
- Obtain present and historical property tax data.
- Order an appraisal of the property.

- Request copies of any current and outstanding mortgages and lender information.
- Contact contractors for any work that may need to be done and get a quote.
- Obtain copies of all operating income and expenses over the last few years.
- Request and craft your real estate pro forma.
- Request documentation of all structural improvements made during the previous five years.
- Obtain salary and payment information for all employees or contracted businesses that service the property.
- Request any currently aged payables and receivable reports.

Legal Standing

- Obtain copies of leases and ensure everything is sound and accurate.
- Check with the owner and the city for any pending litigation.
- Request information regarding any previous lawsuits brought against the property.
- Obtain copies of all warranties.
- Review reports ensuring Americans with Disabilities Act compliance.

- Ensure you have any property licenses, permits, and certificates of city-sanctioned property inspections (fire, health, etc.).
- Request a title report.

Now, with the preliminary stages dealt with, it is time to move towards the matter of money. Let's see how you can come to own multifamily property.

PART - III - IRONING OUT THE FINANCES

10

MAKING THE RIGHT OFFER

C hapters 8, 9, and 10 are separate in this book for the sake of better understanding. By now, I'm sure you've realized that they go hand-in-hand. All of them have been about researching and educating yourself on your property so that you can eventually make an offer.

This chapter will explore what it means to make the right offer and how to go about it.

PREPARING FOR THE OFFER

We're finally here. You've done your due diligence and calculated your capitalization rate and net operating income. Everything looks to be exactly where you want it. Now it's time to make an offer. Sellers are looking to get a deal, and most likely, they are looking to offload their property for the best amount they can. The better the pricing, the more money you can make going in.

The first decision is determining how much you want to offer to pay for the property. Now, of course, you could always look at what the seller is offering and request precisely that. However, you may lose money without researching and making your calculations. This is where all the analyses we've learned come in handy.

Look at the comparables for similar properties in the area. During your due diligence phase, you should have done walkthroughs and drive-bys of various properties in the area and have an average ballpark figure for local properties. The upside is that most of those property values will reflect any inflation and the increase in property value due to community development. The downside is that it does not consider the income of your building or any of the other specific characteristics.

The next thing you'll want to do is make your calculations. Check your capitalization rate as well as estimated net operating income. From Chapter 6, we learned how to use the cap rate and the net operating income to develop a sample sales price. Working with a real estate agent, you can determine the average cap rate for a sample of properties in your area to arrive at a sales price.

It is a good idea to determine the replacement cost of the property in which you're interested. By calculating how much it would take to rebuild a similar building from start to finish, you can get a ballpark replacement cost price.

To do this, use the cost by the square foot method. You determine how much value per square foot a building would have, then multiply by the total square footage. For example, suppose you decide that your property's cost per square foot is $80. In that case, you will multiply $80 by the total square footage of the property you are looking to buy. That's your sales price.

Use these methods to determine your offer price. Once you have a solid number, compare it to the seller's asking price. If yours is a higher number, you may have discovered an opportunity. This circumstance means that you are getting a great deal, or there may be other undisclosed issues about the property. It may be prudent to go back and see if you missed anything during your due diligence. If your number is lower than the asking price, now you get to perform some negotiation.

THE ART OF NEGOTIATION

The art of negotiation has always been a tricky subject, and real estate is no different. It's hard to say what you should or should not do when negotiating. Every single deal is unique, and you'll find that sometimes submitting an offer over the asking price may be more advantageous than lowballing the seller and asking for something cheaper. Remember, the purchase price is only part of the battle, albeit an important one.

Understanding the people you are negotiating with can make your negotiation process more successful. Are they a bank that's trying to offload a foreclosed-upon house? Are they private business owners looking to transfer to a different state? Knowing why your seller is selling their property can give you an advantage during negotiation.

You've done your due diligence by this point, so you probably know the property's general value. Be aware that you will not be the only one determining the value of this property. If you live or purchase property in an area that attracts many investors, you'll want to move quickly and cunningly.

Submitting an offer over the asking price is useful when you're trying to buy a property with a lot of value and opportunity. Perhaps the property is older and has not been updated, but it's in a decent neighborhood and could attract quality tenants. In this case, you'll want to get ahead of other investors.

It helps to have a vision in your mind to know what you can do to improve the property's value or income beforehand. If you can draw up a prospective plan, you can make a case for why you should be paying more on this property than asking. Sometimes moving swiftly and offering a couple thousand over the asking price can be just what the seller needs for you to stand out and for them to decide to strike a deal with you.

Lowballing is useful when you know that a property has been blatantly overpriced and won't attract many other investors. It's also useful when you know that an owner wants to offload the property quickly and be done with it. They will often basically give their property away to whoever gives them money. If the property is sound, it may pay off, in the long run, to submit a lowball offer and get the property for cheaper than asking, particularly if no one else has expressed interest and they've had a hard time selling it.

MAKING OFFERS FOR OFF-MARKET PROPERTIES

Earlier, we mentioned that you could find properties that may not be listed, but the owners are willing to sell. We called these off-market properties. Typically, when someone is selling a property, you give them a call, hash out the details, tour the property, and decide whether you have an interest in the deal.

The seller often wants to talk a little bit to give you an idea of the property, and then they may begin mentioning selling prices. In other cases, you can also send **a letter of intent** where you outline the conditions and parameters of the purchase and sale. With this maneuver, both the seller and buyer can see the offer's overview and what's on the table. A letter of intent is neither a legally binding document nor an official purchase statement, and it's usually just a way to break the ice and begin the conversation.

If the buyer and seller are interested in moving forward, they may consider formulating a purchase and sale agreement. They can get this form from websites that offer legal documents based on state or from a local title company. Either way, they should have their legal professionals review the agreement to ensure it is sound, legally binding, and reflective of the intentions of both parties.

MAKING THE OFFER ON YOUR MULTIFAMILY PROPERTY

When making an offer on a multifamily property, you will need to have a few things ready beforehand. One of those things is the letter of intent to outline terms and conditions. Submitting your letter allows you to mention any issues or agreements you want to make and include in the contract. Usually, if you can agree on the letter of intent, you should have no problem agreeing on the contract.

Another vital thing to consider is **earnest money**. This money is a small deposit to the seller to demonstrate a buyer's intention to purchase a property. Usually, the earnest money is about 1% or more of your purchase price. You'll want to make sure that you know whether the money is refundable or non-refundable.

In your letter of intent, you'll want to include your property price, earnest money, terms of finance, and any issues you found in your due diligence. Make sure you negotiate and communicate the time needed to approve your loan. For loan approvals, you'll need to speak with your loan broker.

Generally, it takes about 30 to 50 days after receiving the loan application for approval. You'll also want to outline the time it'll take for you to close on the deal. The lending procedure usually takes the most time, and a safe bet for closing is around 40 to 70 days.

Suppose you've been investing in multiple properties. In that case, you should also make sure to include that in your letter of intent and any references from your loan broker, attorney, or other relevant professionals so you can speak to your integrity in this process. Proof of cash funds is also beneficial here.

LET'S PRACTICE - LETTER OF INTENT

The letter of intent is a declarative note outlining the buyer's intentions. Usually, it supplies the desired purchase price and other terms and conditions.

Let's take a moment to create a sample letter of intent. I've also included a sample you can reference:

LETTER OF INTENT

123 Sample Street

Random Town, USA

Re: Purchase of 123 Sample Street

Dear [Mr./Mrs. Name]:

I am pleased to submit the following Letter of Intent for [insert your name] to acquire this property from you. This note is to clarify the purchase price we are prepared to pay. Further terms will be set in a formal contract. I want to acquire the property based on the following:

PURCHASE PRICE: $_____

DEPOSIT TO ESCROW AND DUE DILIGENCE: $_____ [if applicable]

CLOSING COSTS: [insert terms of closing costs, including if the seller is expected to pay or the buyer is expected to pay. If closing costs are to be split, indicate how you suggest.]

This is a Letter of Intent and is not a formal binding agreement, even if both parties agree on the terms of the letter. This is an expression of the general terms for the Seller to consider upon entering a binding contract. Please sign and return this letter to [insert email or fax here]

Time is of the essence. This letter is valid until [date] at [time, AM/PM, time zone]

Sincerely,

[your name and any titles or company]

[signature]

Agreed (Buyer)   Agreed (Seller)

_____Date: _____Date:

11

PURCHASING AND FINANCING OPTIONS

S o far, you've been calculating what the property you want to buy is worth and how much money it can potentially make. But once you've decided on the offer—considering your finances—it is time to make sure that you start making the arrangements and set things in motion.

Before financing your property, make sure that your due diligence is complete. It would help if you also decided on **multifamily property insurance**. This insurance will not be as simple as one that you would get for purchasing a primary residence single-family home, and it's going to be notably more expensive. Make sure you know your coverage. You've purchased this property under your name as a property owner, which means you are personally liable for any issues that could arise with the property. Insurance helps offset some of that risk.

As we've mentioned in earlier chapters, multifamily properties usually fall under commercial real estate. However, small multifamily real estate (anything between two to four units) falls under a residential classification. That means you can get a residential loan, which is more accessible and more straightforward to obtain than a commercial loan.

In addition, this means you can potentially get a low-interest loan just by occupying one of the units in your multifamily property. You do this by making your multifamily investment your primary residence and applying for a Federal Housing Administration (FHA) loan. These loans have several advantages, and they are like the loans that many first-time homebuyers will use when purchasing their primary residence.

FINANCING TERMS TO KNOW

Before we continue, there are some key financing terms that you should know. Understanding these terms will simplify navigating the financing and purchase process.

Interest rate: Interest refers to the cost of borrowing money. The interest rate is usually what you pay on top of the money you have already borrowed. It's commonly expressed as a yearly percentage and is included in your monthly loan payment.

Terms: Terms usually refer to a length of time. The duration of an agreement is unique to each deal made and indicates how long the debt will be paid off. In real estate, there are usually long-term loans and short-term loans.

- Short-term loans are usually used to fix a property or obtain a new construction property. Short-term loans range from 6 to 12 months, and conventional sources of financing are generally willing to lend for the short term.
- Long-term loans are what investors use when financing a property. These are usually paid off over 30 years. You can obtain long-term loans at almost any institution that lends to borrowers.

As an additional note, if you are hoping to use what's "normal," there are no typical terms. Everything depends on the specific deal you are trying to close. These terms can vary depending on the agreement you're negotiating, how strong a candidate you are, and why you're borrowing.

Loan Limits: We're thinking about how much you can pull out for a loan when we think about loan limits. Often there isn't anything specific regarding commercial real estate; however, you should be aware that this may change when purchasing a residential multifamily property. Individual banks may also have their limits on what loans they're willing to offer. Sometimes, if the need is significant enough, banks may partner with other banks, or they may do larger individual loans if they are capable.

Loan-to-Value: If someone mentions loan-to-value requirements, they're talking about a way to compare the amount of mortgage to the property's value. A significant benefit of buying a residential multifamily home is that lenders sometimes allow borrowers to put down 20% or less. Sometimes lenders may even let buyers put down 0%, depending on the buyer and the property.

Conventional Financing Options: What we consider conventional refers to several different kinds of lenders. Most commonly, this refers to banks of any kind.

Banks are the number one lender for mortgages but not the only ones. Sometimes life insurance companies can loan to multifamily borrowers, and many even come with low-interest rates.

Agency loans could also be considered conventional and are commonly supported by government-sponsored enterprises like Fannie Mae or Freddie Mac. These often come with an implied guarantee—meaning if the borrower defaults, the government will step in to pay off the debt.

Alternative Financing Options: Sometimes, the traditional route doesn't work out, and borrowers need to explore more creative means of financing the property. You may hear about options like debt funds which are capital used to fund commercial real estate. You may also hear about online marketplaces where various investors add funding, and borrowers have the option to finance their debt.

The riskiest of these alternate lenders is the **hard money lender.** It's a private lender who will hand out short-term loans that usually have very high-interest rates. These are not ideal loans, and you should only explore these if you plan to implement a concrete repayment plan.

OPTIONS FOR FINANCING

Multifamily home investment comes with several different options for financing. The first and most apparent is the conventional mortgage. The bank usually offers these mortgages and qualifies multifamily properties which have between two and four units. These mortgages are outstanding for those small residential properties we are examining here. They must meet specific requirements and have fixed or variable interest rates. The conditions may be rigorous, but typically, you can get the loan with a reasonable interest rate if you have an acceptable credit score and a good down payment.

You may also want to consider a **portfolio loan**. Often property owners will get portfolio loans when trying to finance several properties under one mortgage. These are usually mortgages held primarily by the lender and are not sold to Fannie Mae or Freddie Mac. The criteria that portfolio loans meet differ from typical Federal standards. They can have higher loan-to-value rates and maximum loan size, and higher interest rates and fees often follow these loans.

Government-backed multifamily loans are loans that have the federal government's support behind them. Often, they follow the same guidelines as Fannie Mae, Freddie Mac, and the Federal Housing Administration. These loans usually come with various requirements that the consumer must follow, and FHA multifamily loans fall under this category. We'll spend more time looking at these because they are standard options for new multifamily investors to utilize.

Finally, short-term multifamily financing is helpful when you're trying to renovate or update a property. These include hard money loans that can be risky if you do not have a solid plan to prevent getting sunk by the high-interest rates and repayment.

FINDING A BROKER

As an investor, it's your decision whether you want to work with a multifamily broker. Alternatively, you can go to a lender directly and try to hash out a deal yourself. But using a broker comes with several benefits.

A broker can help you understand what options are best for you and use their relationships to connect you with a lender who best fits your circumstances. More importantly, they can help you with the many confusing and tedious portions of the application process. Often there may be fine-print items, hard-to-understand jargon, or complex documentation.

Brokers may charge a small percentage of the loan amount as payment for their services, but this is usually negligible compared to the headaches you can avoid by utilizing their service.

UNDERSTANDING THE FHA PROCESS

Based on the type of property we've been reviewing in this book, you may be interested in utilizing the FHA loan for your purchase. Therefore, you must understand all the nuances of this financing option.

How the FHA Loan Works

An FHA loan is a government-backed loan built with the intent to assist people who may not be in a suitable financial situation to buy a home. Typically, FHA loans are helpful to people interested in purchasing a single-family home or investors who desire to purchase multifamily dwellings with five units or more. However, many people don't realize that FHA loans can also qualify for multifamily units when the owner is a resident in one of those units.

The property must be in decent condition and not subject to any significant repair work to be eligible. The investor must repair anything crucial found during the inspection within the year, and the building must have been constructed or renovated three or more years before applying.

There are three main types of FHA multifamily loans: the FHA acquisition loan, the FHA construction rehab loan for co-ops, and the FHA construction and rehab loan for condos.

We will only be looking at the FHA multifamily acquisition loan for our purposes.

The FHA multifamily acquisition loan focuses primarily on purchasing or refinancing a property. Loan-to-value tends to range from 83.3% to 87%, and the mortgage term usually does not exceed 35 years. It must also be long enough to allow for a 10-year mortgage. The FHA loan requires as little as a 5% down payment when purchasing multifamily properties.

Where to Find FHA Loans

You can find FHA loans at the most well-known banking institutions. Some significant ones to note include Capital One, J.P. Morgan Chase Bank, Regions Bank, and Wells Fargo. Schedule to speak with a representative to see if you qualify for an FHA loan. Make sure to have all your financial information by then. Show plans to rent out the other units on the property. You may find that lenders are more willing to cooperate because they see that you have multiple income streams from the property.

The FHA multifamily loan process generally follows these six steps:

Step 1: Choose an FHA-approved lender.

Step 2: Fill out the loan application.

Step 3: Qualify for a firm commitment.

Step 4: Receive the FHA mortgage commitment.

Step 5: Confirm that the lender is clear to close.

Step 6: Settlement

Alternatives to FHA Multifamily Loans

While we've spent a lot of time examining FHA multifamily loans, they are not the only means of financing available to multifamily investors.

Veteran Affairs (VA) will also finance buildings containing up to four units if the owner claims to live in one of those units. The VA will qualify the loan based on the total household income, including the net income. Those eligible might get a VA loan for as low as $0 down, even for multifamily homes. But you'd have to make sure that you meet the requirements.

State programs generally follow the same trend as your VA and FHA loans. Again, you will need to live in one of the building units, and the net rental income will be added to your income when you're ready to qualify for the loan. The down payment is low, as are the interest rates—competing with FHA and VA policies.

A more unusual method of financing is to do owner-financing. This is when the seller technically becomes the lender, and instead of getting the total purchase price at closing, they will receive principal and interest payments monthly. Owners often shorten finance terms to around ten years and may request higher interest rates than other lenders. Sellers may do this because they don't require cash at the time of purchase, and they realize that monthly payments are a good source of regular income. Sometimes if the seller is open to this idea, it makes the purchase price more manageable.

NACA MORTGAGE

The Neighborhood Assistance Corporation of America (NACA) helps potential buyers who may not have the funds to become homeowners. They do this through counseling, affordable mortgages, and other services. Anyone who completes the requirements to become NACA-qualified can receive the mortgage. You must be active in your membership to take advantage of these opportunities.

Although there are no extenuating expenses for mortgages, you will need all other requirements for closing on your property, including any earnest money and the down payment. NACA will put a lien on the property to make sure that you live on the property and that you will repay the mortgage. NACA also stipulates that the borrower must meet specific threshold requirements in credit score and debt to income ratio.

The purchase price of your property would not be able to go above whatever the standard zone limit is for that area. Also, your mortgage payment cannot be more than 31% of your gross monthly income. Although you can use these loans for multifamily homes, you, as the owner, will need to be present and residing on the property.

To qualify, you must attend a mandatory workshop held in different cities throughout the month. You will also be required to meet with a housing and financial counselor who will help you go through your finances and decide if you are ready to own the property. You also need to attend a workshop about purchasing your home and the buying process.

Once you decide on a house, you'll have to contact the housing and financial counselor and receive a qualification letter so that you have proof that you can buy the property.

The property must be in good condition for the NACA mortgage to go through, so you will need to receive a home inspection. Finally, you will meet with your mortgage lender to complete the application process. Usually, the mortgage comes from a private lender like a bank or other institution. Once you're a member and follow all the requirements, you'll have access to financial advisors and the membership assistance program, which helps provide guidance and relief due to economic hardship or disaster.

If you don't qualify for NACA, you can also investigate alternate programs like first-time homebuyer programs, down payment assistance, and the National Homebuyer Fund.

TIME TO CLOSE

We've come to the end of the first step of the road. You've decided on your ideal property, examined it, and evaluated it. Now you are ready to finish acquiring your investment, and it's time to close on your property.

During closing, you should have all your affairs in order. Both you and any legal or real estate professional should review the contract before the closing, and there should be no more terms to negotiate. When it comes to a multifamily investment, most title companies can handle the closing. You'll want to make sure that you have a company that knows how to manage investment properties or any property dealing with money like rent and security deposits.

Make sure that any security deposits will transfer to you at closing. Security deposits are not for you to spend; they must sit securely in the bank. These deposits go straight back to the tenants unless some extenuating damages or cleanings need to occur upon their moving out. To help with this, it's usually best practice to keep them in an account separate from any personal or business accounts that you may have.

There you have it, from financing to closing. But instead of going solo or even spending all your money, there are still other ways of financing a multifamily property. Let's look at those options.

12

ALTERNATE INVESTMENT OPTIONS AND HOUSE HACKING

W e will deviate just a bit and talk more about how we can invest in multifamily properties. Sometimes, you may not have the hard capital needed to make a cash offer or even a sizable down payment on a property. But all is not lost. There are still several ways to buy a home with little to no money. You just have to be creative.

STRATEGIES FOR BUYING HOMES WITH NO MONEY

You can use several different strategies when financing a multifamily property with little to no money down. We've covered a few of these in earlier chapters, including Chapter 11. But we'll explore more of these as we enter conversations about alternate investments.

If you find that you can't get a loan approved from a traditional or even a nontraditional lender, sometimes you can try to work with private lenders. These don't have to be organizations or institutions; they can be family, friends, or work colleagues. You might agree that they receive a certain percentage of rent or that you pay a portion of interest during the loan repayment.

Suppose your multifamily property happens to be somewhere you may get environmental benefits, like mineral rights. In that case, you may be able to sell these resources to increase the size of your down payment. Likewise, suppose your multifamily property sits on a large parcel of land. You can sell off an acre or two to generate a larger down payment in that example. Alternatively, lenders may also be willing to give you money in exchange for a part of your land.

As mentioned in Chapter 11, you can also talk to hard money lenders. Even though their interest rates and fees are higher, they are more willing to lend to people who may not fit the traditional requirements for conventional or FHA loans.

A different version of this is to find an equity share investor. You offer them a piece of the equity of your property, and, in exchange, they give you the funds that you need to buy your multifamily home. The percentage share you offer your investor will usually mean that they also get that percentage of the income and any proceeds you get from selling the property. Investors love the idea of passive income, which allows them to indulge.

We'll go into more detail about two powerful strategies: house hacking and real estate crowdfunding. **House hacking** involves renting out part of a property that the owner is currently living in. On the other hand, **crowdfunding** consists of getting small amounts of money from many different investors, eventually adding up to what you need for your considerable investment.

You can also investigate real estate syndication or partnerships. In these arrangements, you partner with another investor who may have better financial resources, and together you buy the multifamily property that interests you. Partners share active roles in property ownership.

CROWDFUNDING REAL ESTATE

As we just mentioned, crowdfunding has to do with collecting smaller fund amounts from various investors. This method allows you to gain more access to funding, connect you with other investors who can be tremendous sources of information, and get your property up and running despite not having the financial capital you usually need.

As stated in Chapter 10 and Chapter 11, when we approach sellers or lenders and state our intent either with a letter or verbally, it helps to have references. Crowdfunding allows us a great way to showcase our credibility to lenders and sellers. By showing them that we have multiple investors in our corner, we not only show that we have the requisite capital behind us, but we also have the accountability and pull of other investors. Crowdfunding is also a great way to find potential tenants and discover great property deals. The more people you know, the more information you receive.

Crowdfunding is not without its challenges, however. Uncertainty is one of the biggest challenges you may face as you try to network and connect with other investors. People want to get to know you before sending money your way. You'll have to earn the trust of your investors, and sometimes that can be challenging, especially if you don't have an excellent track record. Sometimes investors may be skeptical about seeing a return on their investment. It may take time before you can deliver a sizable repayment to those who have so painstakingly poured financial support into your property.

Types of Crowdfunding

There are two main types of crowdfunding. The first is equity investments, which are what investors usually use.

Equity investments mean that investors in a particular property become "shareholders." The return of the investment will then be based on the rent from the property or on whatever percentage the property sale yields. For most investors, the upside to this is that they get tax benefits and could earn a tremendous amount, depending on how well the property does. However, many don't like waiting for the return on their investment. The idea of not being the first one to get paid can also frighten some investors because their recovery depends entirely on how well the property performs.

The second type of investment is **debt investment**. In this case, the investor is the lender to the property owner. You should expect regular returns based on how well the property does and the overall income. These usually have less risk than equity investments, and the returns are consistent. However, some investors struggle because crowdfunding platforms may require them to pay higher fees. There could be a limit to the returns that investors receive—instead of the unlimited returns that equity investments can receive.

Quality Real Estate Crowdfunding Platforms

Trying to find the right crowdfunding platform is a lot like trying to find the right weed killer. There seem to be many of them, and everyone claims that they're the best. While many crowdfunding platforms are decent, three stand out from the others regarding real estate.

DiversyFund is a popular one, especially for people who like REITs. DiversyFund allows investors to get instant access to portfolio investments without managing properties. However, it doesn't allow for early withdrawals, and some investment choices can be somewhat limited. But it also doesn't charge any broker fees, which is a nice benefit.

Fundraise is an excellent first crowdfunding platform for real estate investors if you're just getting into the crowdfunding game. It's an online marketplace, and investments start very low. This platform has allowed tons of people to become property investors. It also has one of the largest networks across the crowdfunding platform world. You don't need any accreditation, and it's simple to use.

CrowdStreet is an excellent platform for those interested in investing in loans. It's usually for accredited investors who want to build a real estate portfolio, and investors can put their money towards private real estate loans. This platform allows lenders to give money to real estate owners, and it subsequently collects monthly payments, after which you get a share of those monthly payments. This platform enables you to diversify your portfolio and customize your investments as you desire. However, it only offers debt investments which means that there can be a higher risk than other crowdfunding options.

PLANNING FOR PARTNERSHIPS

Let's say that you decide to take a different route. Maybe you're not a big fan of technology or prefer to deal with someone in person. A real estate partnership can hold a lot of benefits; however, it also can come with several pitfalls.

First, decide if you even *want* a partner.

Having a partner means that there is a second entity that you must run all your business decisions through.

This person may be able to influence the financial output of your property. Even if this person is not involved, just that person putting their name on a document means that you do not have total and ultimate control of your investment. Knowing your tolerance level is a vital part of beginning a quality partnership. You want to make sure that you're matching yourself with someone who has the same values, goals, and vision.

Finding a suitable partner can be difficult, but not impossible. Often, you can join online forums, meet-up groups, or real estate associations that will put you in close contact with like-minded individuals. Before approaching someone you think might make a great partner, make sure that you do your diligence on this person. Like a property, you are investing time and effort into someone else, and you want to ensure that you get a good return on your investment.

In any successful partnership, you first want to make sure that you set the parameters and boundaries of your relationship. Be confident and comfortable with your decisions. Set the terms and outline how you'll divide the work and the profit. Sometimes that may mean splitting the work and profit 50-50. Other times that may mean that you do more groundwork and run around while your partner puts up the money and bankrolls the endeavor. Whatever your arrangement is, understanding your role and your partner's role is crucial to success.

After determining your roles, make sure you know how to manage the profits. If you are working with someone more seasoned and bringing more resources and networking to the table, you may take a smaller cut based on experience.

Once you've got things arranged, you'll need to make sure that you establish a real estate partnership agreement. It is essential to do this for several reasons. The main reason is to protect you. Should things go south with your partner, you'll need your agreement documentation when entering this partnership. Documenting your agreement also makes sure that you are not financially liable for anything outside the realm of what you've discussed with your financial partner. This framework helps you understand how your business is structured and operated. Included in this agreement should be the responsibilities of each partner—especially if they differ.

Once you establish how you will split the work responsibilities, finances, roles, and responsibilities with your partner and how you will protect each of your assets, you want to draw up a draft of the partnership agreement. Ideally, it's good to have someone who has some legal knowledge to help make sure that this document is sound. At the very least, having another real estate professional look over it can help you avoid any possible hiccups. However, a little money now to hire a professional to look over this document can potentially save significant money down the road.

Partnership vs. Syndication

One less-talked-about form of partnership is a real estate syndication.

Real estate syndication is where multiple investors use their funds jointly to purchase a property. Usually, one person acts as a Sponsor and makes sure to locate the deal and complete the seller's transaction. At the same time, anyone involved in the agreement serves as a passive investor. This type of partnership frequently occurs with multifamily properties and follows the same lines as a typical real estate partnership. It would be best if you still had the same conversations about splitting the work and profit. The investors put money into the property, and the Sponsor does the legwork to close the deal and provide the property.

Like with crowdfunding, the Sponsor or the person doing the legwork will distribute the profit as agreed to the passive investors based on the revenue and property appreciation. Usually, syndications consist of a limited liability company or a limited partnership, while the Sponsor serves as the general partner or manager. An LLC or LP still require a partnership agreement since they outline the rights and roles of sponsors and investors.

Although syndication is somewhat different from a partnership, it still appeals to many investors who want to put money into a property and not have to work on it. That investment can eventually become passive income. You may run into roadblocks when trying to get out of syndication because of the nature of the arrangement. The syndication will hold any funds you invest for a substantial period, and you may not have much impact on the day-to-day handling of the property.

HOUSE HACKING 101

"House hacking" is one of the ideal options for multi-family property owners. You get all the tax benefits from living in your investment as your primary residence, and you also get the benefit of having renters generate income for the property. This same technique allows people who may be low income to live in some of the highest income cities in the nation while building wealth. House hacking offers the added benefits of reducing your housing cost by paying your mortgage based on the rent received, giving you the ability to be flexible, offsetting the risk of property investment, and growing your wealth all along the way.

But how do you get started with house hacking? The good news about this is that you've learned most of it already! You have learned how to find the best property and calculate the capitalization rate and the rate of income. You've also learned how to figure out financing and find the best lender for you. Most importantly, you've learned to run the numbers and can now figure out how much you need to pay for a mortgage and expenses.

House hacking first starts with following the **D.E.A.L.S.** formula. Decide on a home, examine, and value the property, acquire the property, make sure you understand the logistics for that property, and then begin to strategize for the future. Instead of repeating everything you've already learned in the last few chapters, let me give you an example of how to apply it all to house hacking.

Chad Carson is a popular YouTube influencer who spends a lot of time talking about home investments and real estate. House hacking was one of the first ways he got involved in real estate work. As a real estate investor for 17 years, he's benefited from house hacks and lived in one of his early investments for quite some time before eventually moving on.

His first house hack was a foreclosed-on fourplex. The building was trashy, outdated, and desperate for some TLC. But after spending $45,000 and fixing it up, it was finally ready for tenants. He lived in one unit and was able to fill the other three units.

He bought the fourplex for $70,000 using a bank loan and private financing. At the time, he was receiving around $1200 in monthly rental income. After property taxes, insurance, maintenance, and payment on principal and interest, he walked away with $95 per month as a positive cash flow. The value of the property was now $155,000. He was able to borrow $120,000 and pull out 100% of his invested money after six months, allowing him to pay back the mortgage and the renovation cost.

There is tremendous potential in house hacking, and you already know how to do it. All you must do now is find the right tenants and learn to manage your property correctly.

PART - IV - MAINTENANCE AND LONG-TERM STRATEGIES

13

MANAGING YOUR PROPERTY

Once a property is in your hands, you need to ensure that it runs well. Proper management ensures that you keep your units occupied and that the property stays in good condition. At the same time, you increase its valuation and improve the chances of asking for a higher sell price when you're ready to unload it.

PROPERTY MANAGEMENT 101

If you're just starting in the multifamily property business, it's essential to take your time. Once you've purchased your first property, getting excited and taking on too much at once is easy. Start small and learn carefully. It might be helpful to invest in some multifamily management software that can help you with rent collection, advertising, and managing clients and tenants.

Start with establishing ground rules so that people have a reference on behavior expectations. Some tenants may be rowdier than others which could cause a public disturbance and give other tenants a very negative experience. Tenants may also have pets that could be harmful if not kept leashed or restrained somehow. If there is a conflict between tenants, the property manager plays a mediation role—working to resolve things through negotiation.

The Legalities

To legally prepare yourself for property management, start by understanding your local state and county laws. Know what is and is not allowed on the property. You should also be aware of the eviction policy in your area and any local or federal anti-discrimination laws. Your building needs to be kept up to code to not be at risk for any potential lawsuits. The last thing you want is to find yourself in court trying to avoid doling out a lot of money.

Setting the Right Price

Make sure to do the correct calculation to determine the best rent for your property. Consider any updates and the demographics of the area you live. The price should be fair and meet the needs and goals you have for your investment property. It might also be an excellent opportunity to establish other revenue-producing services like laundry facilities, vending machines, or other amenities. Instead of laundry facilities, you can increase rent and include laundry in the units.

Screening and Leasing

Screening and leasing your tenants are among the most important parts of property management. Thanks to technology, it's much easier to market your property and make potential tenants aware that you're out there.

Finding a good tenant requires patience and, as usual, due diligence. Potential tenants should fill out screening questionnaires, and due diligence should be done by requesting credit reports, background checks, and interviewing their current or former landlord. You may want to employ more rigorous requirements when living on site.

Having a quality lease is especially important because it sets the tenant's expectations and ensures your property is meeting the vision you have for it. Every lease should have the names of all tenants in the unit, clear limits on the number of people able to stay in the unit, rental terms, rates, pet deposits and fees, restrictions on illegal activity, and any other repair and maintenance expectations.

The lease is your first clear communication with your tenant. You want to ensure that you are transparent and straightforward in every contact. Do this, and you'll find that most tenants reward you with the same.

Holding on to Your Tenants

There will always be some tenants that you want to leave sooner than they are willing. Likewise, there will be tenants that you want to continue to lease as long as possible. Being upfront and clear about your expectations is the first step to forming a healthy and lasting relationship with your tenants. In addition, you must follow through on your promises to them, handle maintenance issues swiftly, and address any concerns about pests immediately.

Make necessary emergency repairs as soon as you can. You want your tenants to be comfortable in the space you provide them. Remember, while they live on your property, they are under your care. Reward your tenants for following through on their expectations by following through on yours.

Maintenance and Improvement

Maintenance of your rental property begins with regular inspections. As the owner, you should always inspect the unit before a tenant moves in, and, likewise, you should check the unit once they vacate the building. In addition to these inspections, you can also conduct regular reviews of the outside of your property —looking for any signs of wear, tear, element damage, or structural deformity.

Perform appropriate outdoor seasonal maintenance as well. Care might include setting up snow and salting services if your region gets snow or ice during the winter months. Clean out leaf gutters and slippery steps during the fall and spring months. You might be surprised by how refreshed a property appears after something as simple as a pressure washing to remove ordinary dirt and mold buildup.

Maintenance also includes looking for opportunities to improve your property. Installing energy-efficient devices and fixtures like toilets and LED light bulbs can drastically reduce costs while making your property more valuable. These minor upgrades can also be a practical marketing point for tenants who value a greener and more energy-efficient lifestyle.

Remember, a clean and well-maintained property keeps your residents happy. No one wants to live in a trash heap. As a rule of thumb, if you upgrade one unit in any way, it's best to upgrade the rest of them as soon as possible. You don't want renters to feel jealous or ask why somebody else gets better appliances or property upgrades when paying the same rent.

One way to offset this is by offering renters unit upgrades if they are willing to increase the cost of their rent. For more significant upgrades, it can be helpful to split that cost among renters. Massive undertakings such as updating the HVAC system or running new electric wiring throughout the building might be a challenging expense to absorb all at once. But suppose you are intentional about explaining to tenants that the rent will be increased by $50 due to a new, efficient HVAC system that will improve safety for everyone. In that case, most renters are willing to work with you.

Property maintenance at its best is preventative, and taking regular care of your property can keep it from falling into disrepair. If you see any potential problems, resolve them as soon as possible. Being responsive reduces complaints from tenants and makes sure that your property remains a sound investment.

There will be times when things break or fall apart, either because the tenant has had an accident or something unexpected. You often cannot predict where the pipe will burst or if the next-door neighbor's kid will throw a baseball through the window of one of your bottom floor units. These are unexpected expenses, and sometimes things just happen.

When a tenant issues a complaint or concern, make sure you record it so you can easily access the information if the tenant raises it again. Also, note how you addressed the matter and when and who managed it.

All this data is essential so that you can respond quickly to any tenant report. It also allows you to record where the deficiencies in your property may be. For example, if you had to fix a pipe in one unit that burst because of age, you may want to consider updating piping in all the other units. That way, you can prevent further problems and extenuate payments for expensive repairs.

FINANCIAL MANAGEMENT

Fees and Expenses

Financial management is a crucial skill for any good property manager. To assist you with this, you need to know how to find the operating expense ratio. For this equation, you take the total operating expenses, including taxes, insurance, utilities, repairs, marketing, and anything else you must pay to make your property successful. Then you divide this by the gross income.

Operating Expense Ratio = Operating Expenses/Gross Operating Income

You get the operating expense ratio once you've divided the operating expenses by the gross income. A percentage usually depicts this ratio. A lower operating expense ratio usually means that a property is on target and is running well. However, having a higher operating expense ratio implies room for improvement at your property. You may want to make a regular comparison every year to determine if there's any poor spending, old equipment, or if there are services that need eliminating. Usually, you'd like your expense ratio to fall somewhere between 35 and 45%, but that can vary based on your region.

Remember that operating expenses are usually around 50% of the income. We base this on the 50% rule discussed in Chapter 11, and anything too far below that number may indicate an issue.

If you decide to enlist a property management company or another private property manager, you must consider management fees. Those fees are usually an agreed-upon percentage of the property income—

often 10%. Keep in mind that when hiring and working with a management company, you want to make sure that you get someone who knows what they're doing. Don't be afraid to pay competitive prices because it could cost you a lot more down the road if you try to cut corners here.

Increasing Cash Flow

This multifamily property is your investment. The purpose of your investment is to make a profit. So, any way you can increase your cash flow means getting more money in your pocket.

One of the best and most obvious ways to get a good cash flow is to **set an excellent rental rate.** You should base your rent on several different factors. Those factors should be your location and the rental rates of other comparable properties in your area. Ensure you're paying attention to the kind of neighborhood, the number of bedrooms and bathrooms, and whether this is a new or old property.

You can also set the price based on your property's amenities. Suppose your property has excellent updates (for example, granite countertops, new flooring, or laundry in the unit). In that case, you may be able to demand a higher rent. The same goes for any extra closet, square footage, or view that makes the property stand out. Your rental rate might be out of line if you've consistently marketed your property, but no one calls to view it. Take some time to reevaluate the rate you have set. Make sure that it is fair and attractive to potential tenants. The last thing you want is a vacancy for an extended period, causing you to lose money.

Another way that you can increase your cash flow is by **decreasing your operating expenses**. That means cutting off any unnecessary services, going with cheaper, more affordable services, and trying to find deals on any materials or supplies needed to improve your property. In addition, you can increase the value of your rent or property by furnishing the unit for people who plan on a short-term lease or just don't want to buy their furnishings. You can also add laundry services, vending machines, and other options to increase your revenue sources.

You can also work on your loans. You can get better terms and decrease the interest you're paying on your mortgage by refinancing a loan. You can also put all your money towards paying off your loan as soon as possible so that you're no longer paying interest and decreasing the debt you owe. Less debt means more money in your pocket.

You can use any low-cost debt to purchase new investments to grow your portfolio along the same lines. By doing that, you're increasing your cash flow by pulling out the equity in your property to buy new properties. If you feel as though the current debt you have has interest rates that are too high, you can also pull equity out to pay off the debt with the highest interest rates to save more over the long run.

The approaches here are only the tip of the iceberg. There are many more tricks and skills that property managers utilize to help their property become successful. Investigate and consider what works best for you and your property.

Now we've got a successful property purchased affordably and filled with happy tenants. All that's left is what you choose to do with your property in the long term. This final chapter will cover some basic investment strategies you can use for your property.

14

LONG-TERM STRATEGIES FOR WEALTH-BUILDING

You're now a multifamily investor. But the journey doesn't stop there. With growth potential at your fingertips, it's time to decide how to use your property to your advantage. This final chapter will cover some basic investment strategies you can use for your property.

INVESTING STRATEGIES

Value Add

We'll go into more detail on this one later. However, one of the most popular ways to invest in your property long-term is to find a value-add property. Investors commonly use this to buy a property that's been outdated or needs some light cosmetic upgrades, make those changes, and turn around and sell it for a profit. You can also increase the value of a property by optimizing its property management structure, manipulating debt to decrease interest rates or payments, or simply creating a better lease structure for tenants. Investors have a moderate risk, which stems from the improvements and capital needed to make those upgrades for the property.

Opportunistic

Opportunistic investments can be very challenging, but they also offer one of the most excellent opportunities for a return. There are several different kinds of opportunistic strategies. One main one is to take the **value-add strategy to the extreme**. It means buying a property that is a dump and using that opportunity to invest a lot of capital.

This strategy is risky because you are taking on a property that may not even see a return for quite some time, especially if you cannot get a tenant to move in. These properties can often come with many significant structural deficiencies.

Even riskier is **buying a property in an area that you hope will develop further.** You may purchase multiple multifamily homes in an area that is currently not favorable but shows signs of someday becoming a better neighborhood. So, you are counting on that projection to pay off later. You purchase the property very cheaply now and, over time, see greater and greater returns as the area develops and more people or businesses move in.

Core/Core-Plus

Core investments are very much the opposite of value-add and opportunistic investments. These investments are usually newer buildings constructed within the last ten years and are in a stable market with high-income potential and excellent tenant access. These properties will be the more stabilized properties and give investors a more confident return on their investment.

Core-plus, however, is a combination of value-add and core strategies. This strategy is where an investor will find a property that has the potential to be improved with cosmetic or operational improvements but is still a quality, low-risk property. Usually, these are class A and class B multifamily properties.

THE BRRRR METHOD

The BRRRR method stands for: **Buy, Rehab, Rent, Refinance, Repeat**. This method is a standard investment strategy for many new investors in multifamily real estate. There are many different opinions on how effective this method is, but it's popular because it generally works. As a long-term strategy, it is also sound.

The overall idea for this method is to get back the initial investment and put it towards another property. This maneuver allows you to build a portfolio of cash-flowing properties after obtaining your first property. You'll need to develop a buy-and-hold mindset to pull this off.

You're not flipping this property. You are investing, putting in time and money, then holding it so that you can feed your portfolio.

The first step is to buy your property, preferably something with some upside. You'll probably want to consider a value-add property in the B or C class range, and this allows you to get a solid property that still has room for improvement. People generally use financing for this property. You'll have to put down around 20% unless you go with a different financing method like an FHA loan or a NACA agreement (Remember: to qualify for those, you will need to live in that property).

After purchasing your home, you can put money into it and rehab it. Add value by adding amenities, improving the flooring, and updating the appliances, bathrooms, and other rooms. Once you complete rehabilitating your property, you can begin the rental phase of this method.

You have already learned how to find good tenants from our previous chapters. Now you will implement that skill to draw tenants to you who will make good renters. You'll also utilize your property management techniques learned in the last chapter to manage your property. You'll be aiming to get a good cash flow from this process.

The last official step in this method involves refinancing the property. Make sure that you research and determine which bank or lender will be the best option for you. Some banks offer a cash-out refinance, while others will only pay off any outstanding debt. Some banks are also willing to refinance as soon as you have performed rehab on the property and rented it out, while others may require a waiting period of up to a year. Usually, you can refinance up to about 75% of whatever the property's appraised value is.

Now you can take out a new term loan. You can use this term loan to pay off your previous loan and the amount you invested for the down payment and rehabilitation. Not only will you recoup the amount that you initially invested for the down payment and the repair, but chances are you can put money leftover towards another real estate property. Remember that you are still getting income from the previous first investment while doing the same thing on a new property.

Let's gain some clarity with an example:

Let's say you find a class C duplex home for $110,000. You choose to live on the property and make it your primary residence. You qualify to finance the home with an FHA loan for 80% of the cost. So, you put $22,000 in down payment and an extra $1000 for closing costs.

You now owe the bank $88,000 in the mortgage. Your mortgage payment is $1100 per month. You've also paid $23,000 upfront for the property. You then put $6000 in rehabilitation and renovation of the property, and it takes you about a month to complete. You've now paid $29,000 upfront for the property and an extra $1100 for the mortgage.

You rent out the property to another tenant for $1000 per month. You then get an appraisal, and the home value comes back as $160,000. So, you increased your home value by $50,000 by making your updates!

Now you can refinance your home. Let's assume you get the 75% and thus receive a loan for $120,000. You first pay off your mortgage, leaving you with $32,000. You can then use the remainder to recoup your down payment, renovation, and one-month mortgage. You now have around $2,000 in remaining available cash.

Now, that's a pretty good deal! And you're still receiving income from the renter (which no longer needs to apply to the mortgage!). The final step in this method is to repeat the process on another property.

This strategy is a great way to develop a real estate portfolio. This method can be performed on most properties but is especially effective for multifamily properties due to the multiple rents increasing the overall net income.

CONCLUSION

So, that's it. You now have everything you need to start your journey as a multifamily real estate investor. I know what you're thinking: whatever happened to our $250,000 duplex from Chapter 3? It's still there, ready for one last example.

You're a brand new multifamily real estate investor who just read an informational book on multifamily real estate investing. You put the book down and immediately implement the **D.E.A.L.S.** method.

You start by **D**eciding on a property. You scour the newspaper and online listing sites and start attending local real estate meetings. You collect information on the local demographics, average property values, crime rates, and population data. You classify your properties as B or C class properties. After a while, you've got a shortlist of potential properties.

It's time to Evaluate. You use cap rate calculations and the 1% rule to weed out some poor investments. You narrow it down to two properties that look pretty good. You visit the area, check out the neighborhood, and determine how much potential is in the property from public records. One duplex especially stands out. As part of your due diligence, you go to the current owner or broker and request more information on the property's legal, physical, and financial status.

Your $250,000 duplex checks all the boxes! Time to Acquire the property. You prepare your offer, work with a real estate agent, and find the perfect FHA loan for your house hacking strategy. Due to some minor issues, you convince the seller to set the purchase price to $230,000. You offer up $30,000 as a down payment and finance the other $200,000. With a 5% interest rate, your mortgage payment comes to about $1100/month. You can obtain the property!

You decide to follow the BRRR method and immediately invest $5000 into the property to update and make a few changes. Then you do your due diligence to attract, screen, and approve a tenant. Based on the comparable prices in the area, and since you know that you are planning to invest in other properties, you set your tenant's rent to $1100/month. Having just one tenant, you decide to forgo a property management service and handle the management processes yourself. These are the Logistics. All figured out.

You can rehab the property within a month and decide to refinance. The bank does an appraisal on the property, now worth $315,000. You refinance for 75% of the property value and get $236,250. After paying off the mortgage, you then have $36,250 left. After recouping your down payment, closing cost ($1000), and rehab investment, you have $250 cash left over. Now you have Strategies in place for the future of your portfolio!

You've paid off this investment, currently have cash flow from the tenant renting from you, and you're in a great place to start a new investment property. Congrats, you are a real estate investor!

As you've read this book, you may be thinking this sounds relatively simple. Investing can be simple, but it's not always easy. Various unknown problems can arise when taking any risk, no matter how secure. However, you must ask yourself—do the benefits of passive income, financial freedom, and building wealth outweigh these risks? I'll let you be the judge of that. In any endeavor, you should always double-check with a financial advisor or real estate professional before making a significant financial decision.

Real estate remains a lucrative arena for investors, and multifamily homes give you an excellent steppingstone to launch yourself into this field. Working with real estate to build capital is something anyone can get into if pursued strategically. If you enjoyed this book and found the process of starting your multifamily home journey helpful, consider leaving a review on Amazon. I'd love to know how your journey to financial freedom progresses.

ANSWERS TO CHAPTER 6 CAP RATE PRACTICE

You're interested in a triplex property that costs $400,000. Your desired cap rate is above 7%. After speaking with the current owners and investigating, you can determine that the net operating expenses are about $20,000 per year. Calculating for cap rate, will this property meet your target cap rate?

Cap Rate = Net Operating Income/Market Value of Asset

($20,000/$400,000) x 100 = 5%

This will not meet your target cap rate.

You're interested in a triplex property that costs $400,000. Your desired cap rate is above 7%. After speaking with the current owners and investigating, you can determine that the net operating expenses are about $20,000 per year. Calculating for cap rate, will this property meet your target cap rate?

Net Operating Income/Cap Rate = Sale Price

Net Operating Income = Total Annual Revenue - Annual Net Operating Expenses

(NOI = $57600 - $15000 = $42,600) $42,600/.08 = $532,500

GLOSSARY

Amenities - feature or utility supplied in a desirable property

Amortization - payment addressing both principal loan and interest rate at the same time

Appraisal - the assessment and valuation of a property

Appreciation - the amount that a property value increases over time

Capitalization (Cap) rate - the rate used to determine the value of a property

Cashflow - the flow of money in and out of a property as a result of expenses and income

Closing - the completion of the property transaction when the title is conferred to the buyer

Commercial Real Estate - larger scale properties and businesses with the primary purpose of profit

Comparables - similar properties in structure, value, and amenities that can be used to establish value in a property

Creditor - a person who is owed a debt

Default - to not fulfill a contract or responsibility

Depreciation - loss of property value

Disclosure - to reveal unknown facts about a property

Diversification - the practice of spreading out investments across various sectors

Down Payment - an amount of the purchase price paid upfront at closing.

Due Diligence - a period for a buyer to evaluate all aspects of a property

Earnest Money - a small percentage deposit to the seller to demonstrate a buyer's intention to purchase a property

Equity - the stake a homeowner has in their house as revealed by the difference between a home's value and the current mortgage amount

Escrow - a trust arrangement where parties deposit their money

Eviction - the forcible removal of a tenant by law enforcement

Federal Housing Administration (FHA) - a government entity that insures mortgage loans made by lenders

Financial Freedom - obtaining the economic independence needed to live the life one desires

Financial Portfolio - a person's collection of various investments, accounts, and cash

Gross Income - the total income amount before expenses and debts are deducted

Inflation - the increase of prices over time

Interest - the sum paid over time as a fulfillment of the cost of borrowing money

Leverage - using borrowed funds to put towards an investment

Lease - an agreement made between two parties regarding how a property is to be used

Lien - any monetary claims against a property

Loan Limit - how much you can pull out for a loan

Loan-to-Value - a way to compare the amount of mortgage to the value of the property

Mortgage - a contract regarding a loan that was supplied to a borrower and the amount to be paid back

Mortgage-Backed Security (MBS) - an investment consisting of a collection of home loans

Multiple Listing Service (MLS) - any system where real estate organizations post listings about various real estate opportunities

Principal - the amount of a loan owed to the lender that does not include interest

Real Estate Investment Trusts (REITs) - companies that own and/or finance income-generating real estate

Refinancing - the process of restructuring a home loan to get another with a lower interest rate

Rehabilitation - the process of preparing a property to be ready for tenants

Security Deposit - a payment required by a property manager to ensure that a tenant holds to the terms of the lease and takes care of the property

Syndication - a partnership between two or more real estate investors

Tenant - anyone who rents and resides in a property

Title - refers to the right to own a property (usually a document declaring ownership)

Useful Life - a period in reference to how property wears out and decays (usually 27.5 years for residential properties)

Vacancy - an unoccupied unit or property

Walkthrough - the process of inspecting a property before closing

Wholesaling - the process of putting a home under contract and selling the contract to an interested investor

REFERENCES

Assad, A. (n.d.). *How do I manage a multifamily housing complex?* Home Guides | SF Gate. Retrieved April 8, 2022, from https://homeguides.sfgate.com/manage-multifamily-housing-complex-8230.html

Braverman, B. (2020, November 19). *What is a multi-family home?* Bankrate. https://www.bankrate.com/real-estate/what-is-a-multi-family-home/

Bykhovskaia, J. (2019, August 5). *Council post: Five key criteria to evaluate when doing multifamily real estate market analysis.* Forbes. https://www.forbes.com/sites/forbesrealestatecouncil/2019/08/15/five-key-criteria-to-evaluate-when-doing-multifamily-real-estate-market-analysis/?sh=775cb674fb67

Cauble, T. (2020, May 6). *How to: The commercial BRRRR*. The Cauble Group. https://www.tylercauble.com/blog/the-commercial-brrrr

Dehan, A. (2022, January 11). *What Is A Multi-Family Home?* Www.quickenloans.com. https://www.quickenloans.com/learn/what-is-a-multi-family-home

Demeter, R. (2018, September 3). *How to Evaluate the Price of a Multifamily Property*. PropertyShark Real Estate Blog. https://www.propertyshark.com/Real-Estate-Reports/6-easy-steps-for-evaluating-the-price-of-a-multifamily-property/

DiLallo, M. (2022, April 5). *How to invest in real estate*. The Motley Fool. https://www.fool.com/investing/stock-market/market-sectors/real-estate-investing/

ElGenaidi, D. (2021, November 8). *How to evaluate multifamily properties for the highest ROI*. Leverage.com. https://leverage.com/assets/how-to-evaluate-multifamily-properties/

Fairless, J. (2018, May 29). *Guide to real estate due diligence | Apartment deals*. Joe Fairless. https://joefairless.com/ultimate-guide-performing-due-diligence-apartment-building/

Farrington, R. (2018, April 9). *How to get started with house hacking to build wealth.* The College Investor. https://thecollegeinvestor.com/21741/house-hacking/

Greene, D. (2018, December 4). *House hacking: How financially savvy people live in expensive markets while saving money.* Forbes. https://www.forbes.com/sites/davidgreene/2018/12/04/house-hacking-how-financially-savvy-people-live-in-expensive-markets-while-saving-money/?sh=7c5faaf670f0

Hanson, M. (2019, June 7). *Average cost of college [2020]: Yearly tuition + expenses.* EducationData. https://educationdata.org/average-cost-of-college

Harris, J. (2017). *5 reasons why real estate is a great investment.* Entrepreneur. https://www.entrepreneur.com/article/304860

Jonathan. (2021, October 1). *BRRRR calculator + examples to learn how to do the brrrr method • parent portfolio.* Parent Portfolio. https://parentportfolio.com/brrrr-method/

Kearns, D. (2020, June 16). *NACA mortgage: What it is and how it works.* LendingTree. https://www.

lendingtree.com/home/mortgage/what-is-a-naca-mortgage/

Lokboj, T. (2021, October 14). *How to buy a multifamily property - An investor's guide.* Holdfolio. https://holdfolio.com/buy-multifamily-property/

Mansur, N. (2018, March 2). *What is cap rate in real estate investing? A simple guide.* Investment Property Tips | Mashvisor Real Estate Blog. https://www.mashvisor.com/blog/what-is-cap-rate-real-estate-investing/

Merrill, T. (n.d.). *Multifamily Real Estate For Beginners | Than Merrill.* Www.thanmerrill.com. https://www.thanmerrill.com/multifamily-real-estate-investing/

Palmer, B. (2019). *Key reasons to invest in real estate.* Investopedia. https://www.investopedia.com/articles/mortgages-real-estate/11/key-reasons-invest-real-estate.asp

Paskover, M. (2021, January 19). *Everything you need to know about multifamily financing.* Trion Properties. https://trionproperties.com/real-estate-investment-education/articles/everything-you-need-to-know-about-multifamily-financing/

Patterson, M. (2019, November 1). *Buying a duplex, triplex, or fourplex—the ultimate guide.* Fit Small Business. https://fitsmallbusiness.com/how-to-buy-a-duplex-triplex-fourplex/

Salerno, C. (2021, December 2). *Ultimate guide to multifamily real estate syndication - QC capital.* Www.qccapitalgroup.com. https://www.qccapitalgroup.com/post/ultimate-guide-to-multifamily-real-estate-syndication

Schmergel, D. (2020, October 30). *How to conduct due diligence on a multifamily asset.* LoopNet. https://www.loopnet.com/learn/how-to-conduct-due-diligence-on-a-multifamily-asset/1854311490/

September 30, R. H. |, & PM, 2020 at 04:47. (2020, September 30). *6 tips for tackling multifamily due diligence right now.* GlobeSt. https://www.globest.com/2020/09/30/6-tips-for-tackling-multifamily-due-diligence-right-now/?slreturn=20220307221948

The best cities to buy multifamily property in 2022. (2021, December 9). Crexi Insights. https://www.crexi.com/insights/the-best-cities-to-buy-multifamily-property-in-2022

Tiemann, A. (2020, July 20). *Council post: Multifamily due diligence: Eight things most investors miss.* Forbes. https://www.forbes.com/sites/forbesrealestatecouncil/2020/07/20/multifamily-due-diligence-eight-things-most-investors-miss/?sh=48e477146b67

Understanding residential duplexes, triplex, and fourplexes | Chicotsky real estate group. (n.d.). Www.chicotsky.com. https://www.chicotsky.com/services/residential/residential-duplexes-triplex-and-fourplexes

Waterworth, K. (2022, February 22). *The basics of investing in real estate.* The Motley Fool. https://www.fool.com/investing/stock-market/market-sectors/real-estate-investing/basics/

White, S. (2018, April). *13 items to check when purchasing multifamily properties | blog.* Www.biggerpockets.com. https://www.biggerpockets.com/blog/performing-due-diligence-multifamily-properties-checklist

Wichter, Z. (2021, November 8). *How to finance a duplex or multifamily home.* Bankrate. https://www.bankrate.com/mortgages/how-to-finance-a-duplex-or-multifamily-home/